HATCHMENTS IN BRITAIN

5

Kent, Surrey and Sussex

5

Kent, Surrey and Sussex

Edited by

PETER SUMMERS, F.S.A.

and John Titterton

PHILLIMORE

1985

Published by
PHILLIMORE & CO. LTD.
London and Chichester

Head Office: Shopwyke Hall,
Chichester, Sussex, England

ISBN 0 85033 535 3

Typeset in the United Kingdom by:
Fidelity Processes - Selsey - Sussex

Printed and bound in Great Britain by
OXFORD UNIVERSITY PRESS

CONTENTS

ILLUSTRATIONS

GENERAL INTRODUCTION

Hatchments are a familiar sight to all those who visit our parish churches. They are not only decorative, but of great interest to the herald, genealogist and local historian. It is therefore surprising that — apart from local surveys in a few counties mostly in recent years — no attempt has yet been made to record them on a national scale. This series will, it is hoped, remedy the deficiency; it is proposed to publish separate volumes covering all English counties as well as Wales, Scotland and Ireland.

It is probable that no volume will be complete. Previously unrecorded hatchments will turn up from time to time; many have already been found in obscure places such as locked cupboards and ringing chambers. There are likely to be some inaccuracies, for hatchments are often hung high up in dark corners, and the colours may have faded or be darkened with age and grime. Identification is a problem if the arms do not appear anywhere in print: and even if the arms are identified, pedigrees of the family may not always be available. But enough has been done to make publication worth while; the margin to the pages will perhaps allow for pencilled amendments and notes.

Since I began the survey in 1952 many hatchments, probably evicted at the time of Victorian restorations, have been replaced in the churches when they came. On the other hand, during the same period just as many hatchments have been destroyed. An excuse often made by incumbents is that they are too far gone to repair, or that the cost of restoration is too great. Neither reason is valid. If any incumbent, or anyone who has the responsibility for the care of hatchments which need attention, will write to me, I shall be happy to tell him how the hatchments may be simply and satisfactorily restored at a minimal cost. It is hoped that the publication of this survey will help to draw attention to the importance of these heraldic records.

The diamond-shaped hatchment, which originated in the Low Countries, is a debased form of the medieval achievement — the shield, helm, and other accoutrements carried at the funeral of a noble or knight. In this country it was customary for the hatchment to be hung outside the house during the period of mourning, and thereafter be placed in the church. This practice, begun in the early 17th century, is by no means entirely obsolete, for about 80 examples have so far been recorded for the present century.

Closely allied to the diamond hatchment, and contemporary with the earlier examples, are rectangular wooden panels bearing coats of arms. As some of these bear no inscriptions and a black/white or white/black background, and as some otherwise typical hatchments bear anything from initials and a date to a long inscription beginning 'Near here lies buried . . .', it will be appreciated that it is not always easy to draw a firm line between the true hatchment and the memorial panel. Any transitional types will therefore also be listed, but armorial boards which are clearly intended as simple memorials will receive only a brief note.

With hatchments the background is of unique significance, making it possible to tell at a glance whether it is for a bachelor or spinster, husband or wife, widower or widow. These different forms all appear on the plate immediately following this introduction.

Royal Arms can easily be mistaken for hatchments, especially in the West Country where they are frequently of diamond shape and with a black background. But such examples often bear a date, which proves that they were not intended as hatchments. Royal hatchments, however, do exist, and any examples known will be included.

All hatchments are in the parish church unless otherwise stated, but by no means are they all in churches; many are in secular buildings and these, if they have no links with the parish in which they are now found, are listed at the end of the text. All hatchments recorded since the survey began are listed, including those which are now missing.

As with the previous volumes much work has been done in the past by many friends; their records have proved invaluable and greatly lessened the amount of research needed. As for those now responsible for each county who have checked and added to all these early records, I am most grateful for their care and efficiency. For this volume I have been much helped by John Titterton, who is now Assistant Editor, but who will be co-Editor for the remaining volumes of the series.

The illustrations on the following two pages are the work of the late Mr. G. A. Harrison and will provide a valuable 'key' for those unfamiliar with the complexity of hatchment backgrounds.

One last, but important note. Every copy sold of this book helps a child in the Third World; for I have irrevocably assigned all royalties on the entire series to a Charity, The Ockenden Venture.

PETER SUMMERS
Day's Cottage, North Stoke, Oxford

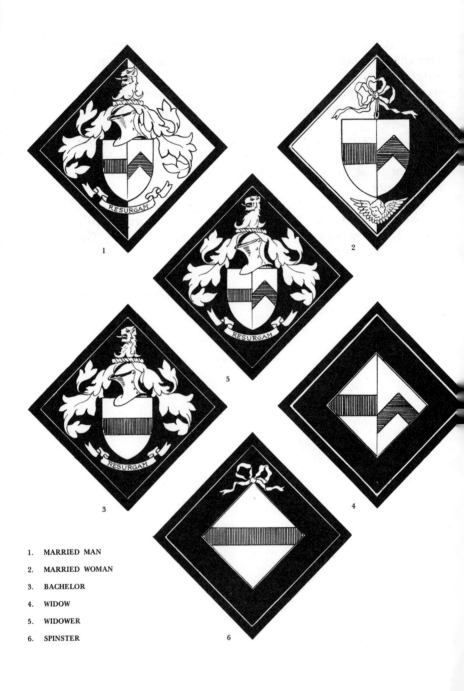

1. MARRIED MAN
2. MARRIED WOMAN
3. BACHELOR
4. WIDOW
5. WIDOWER
6. SPINSTER

1

2

5

3

4

RESURGAM

RESURGAM

6

, 3 and 4—
FOR A MAN
SURVIVING
TWO WIVES

FOR A BISHOP

FOR A PEER OF
THE REALM

ABBREVIATIONS

B.P.	=	Burke's *Peerage, Baronetage and Knightage*
B.L.G.	=	Burke's *Landed Gentry*
B.E.P.	=	Burke's *Extinct and Dormant Peerages*
B.E.B	=	Burke's *Extinct and Dormant Baronetcies*
V.C.H.	=	*Victoria County History*
D.N.B.	=	*Dictionary of National Biography*
M.I.	=	Monumental Inscription
P.R.	=	Parish Register
M.O.	=	*Musgrave's Obituary*
G.M.	=	*Gentleman's Magazine*
Gen. Mag.	=	*Genealogists' Magazine*
M.G. & H.	=	*Miscellanea Genealogica et Heraldica*
O.H.S.	=	Orpington Historical Society
Berry	=	*Berry's County Genealogies*
B. & B.	=	Brayley and Britton

NOTE

Blazons throughout are exactly as noted at the time of recording, not as they ought to be.

KENT

by

R. Bond

Margate 4: For Sir Thomas Staines, 1830
(Photograph by Mr. David Keep)

INTRODUCTION

Kent, with its 344 recorded hatchments has the largest number of all the counties, the earliest being for Valentine Norton at Fordwich, who died in 1650, and the latest for Sir Arthur Luxmoore at Bilsington, who died in 1944.

The survey of the county began in 1952 and, as usual, by the time of the latest check, some hatchments have disappeared. Such a case is Upper Hardres where the collection of seven, which were removed for safe keeping during restoration work in the church, mysteriously disappeared, and are believed to have been destroyed. Some others, unwanted in the churches, are now in Maidstone Museum.

By kind permission of Lord Sackville, the previously unrecorded hatchments at Knole are now included. Some of these are duplicated in Withyham church, Sussex; one of particular interest is for Arabella Cope, who married first, John, 3rd Duke of Dorset, and secondly, Charles, Earl Whitworth. Her arms are shown on two lozenges, impaled with the arms of her two husbands, each surmounted by a coronet of her rank. Even more elaborate is the hatchment of her second husband, Lord Whitworth, at Sevenoaks, which bears two cartouches and a lozenge. The hatchment of Sarah Whatman at Loose is most unusual, for it is circular, within a narrow black frame.

Local families are well represented, notably at Otford, Chevening and Lynsted; and at Chiddingstone where there are ten Streatfeild hatchments. The hatchment of the great Duke of Wellington may be seen at Walmer; there is also a hatchment for him at Stratfieldsaye in Hampshire. As for the unusually large number in Margate parish church some are for residents, but others of which most have not been identified are probably for visitors who came to the town for health reasons and died there.

There are also a number of rectangular and hatchment-type panels; some of the latter, for reasons explained in the

3

main text, are included, but details of the others will appear in a later volume dealing with all transitional examples.

I should like to record my thanks to Miss M. Tester of the Orpington Historical Society, for providing me with the details of their survey, to my wife for suffering many interruptions to her sketching to decipher a colour and to Mrs. P. Froggatt for clearing up the tail-enders which I had been forced to leave.

R. Bond,
Wensheda, Clapper Green, Hunton

ASHFORD

1. Sinister background black
Two shields   Dexter, within the collar of the Order of the Bath and
badge pendent, Qly, 1st, Vert a chevron engrailed between three lions
passant guardant or (Smythe), 2nd, Gules a fess raguly between
three bears' heads couped argent langued azure (Judd), 3rd, Azure
three lions rampant argent langued gules within a bordure argent
(Chich), 4th, Vert a chevron between three eagles displayed or crowned
gules (Fineaux)   Sinister, within an ornamental wreath, Smythe,
impaling, Or ermined sable a cross gules in the first quarter a lion
rampant azure langued gules (Burke)
Viscountess's coronet   Mantle: Gules and ermine   Supporters:
Dexter, A lion rampant or gutty sable langued gules   Sinister, A
leopard argent gutty sable langued gules, chained and collared sable
For Ellen, dau. of Sir Thomas Burke, 1st Bt. of Marble Hill, who
m. 1817, Percy, 6th Viscount Strangford, and d. 26 May 1826. He d.
29 May 1855.   (B.P. 1875 ed.)

AYLESFORD

1. All black background
On a lozenge surmounted by a countess's coronet
Argent a chevron between three griffins passant sable langued gules
(Finch), impaling, Qly, 1st and 4th, Or on a pile gules between six
fleurs-de-lys three and three in pale azure three lions passant guardant
in pale or (Seymour Augmentation), 2nd and 3rd, Gules two wings
conjoined in lure tips downwards or (Seymour)
Supporters: Dexter, A griffin sable ducally gorged or   Sinister, A
lion rampant or
For Charlotte, dau. of Charles, 6th Duke of Somerset, who m. 1750,
Heneage, 3rd Earl of Aylesford, and d. 15 Feb. 1805.
(B.P. 1963 ed.)

2. Dexter background black
Qly, 1st and 4th, Sable three snafflebits or (Milner), 2nd and 3rd,
Azure a chevron between three covered cups or (Butler)
In pretence: Or two pallets gules a chief vair (Belcher)
Crest: A snafflebit or   Mantling: Gules and argent
Motto: I shall rise again
For the Rev. Joseph Milner of Preston Hall, who m. Sarah Belcher,
and d. 26 July 1784. She d. 27 Sept. 1803.   (M.I.)

BADLESMERE

1. Dexter background black
Ermine a millrind between two martlets in pale sable, on a chief engrailed azure two marlions' wings conjoined or (Milles), impaling, Ermine on a cross engrailed between four eagles displayed gules five cinquefoils or (Stracey)
Coronet (not an earl's)   Supporters: Dexter, A griffin argent, beaked and ducally gorged or   Sinister, A bear proper, muzzled argent, collared with a belt buckled, the strap pendent argent, charged with two crescents or, the buckle and strap edges or   Motto: Esto quod esse videris
For George Watson, 1st Earl Sondes, who m. 1859, Charlotte (d. 23 June 1927), eldest dau. of Sir Henry Stracey, 5th Bt., and d. 10 Sept. 1894.   (B.P. 1949 ed.)

BEXLEY

1. All black background
Per pale gules and azure three stags' heads erased and attired or (Lewin), impaling, Vert a chevron embattled counterembattled or (Hale)
Crest: A stag trippant qly or and vert   Mantling: Gules and argent
Motto: Resurgam
For Thomas Lewin, who m. Mary, dau. of Major-General Hale, and d. 1837.   (O.H.S.)

2. Dexter background black
Or a chevron cotised between three griffins' heads couped the two in chief respectant vert (Smith), impaling, Per chevron embattled or and vert three martlets counterchanged (Hodgson)
Crest: An elephant's head erased or eared gules, charged on the neck with three fleurs-de-lys two and one vert   Mantling: Gules and argent   Motto: Tenax in fides
For Oswald Smith, of Blendon Hall, who m. 1824, Henrietta Mildred, dau. of the Very Rev. Robert Hodgson, D.D., Dean of Carlisle, and d. 18 June 1863.   (B.L.G. 1937 ed.)

3. Sinister background black
Qly, 1st and 4th, qly i. & iv. Argent a fess between three mascles sable (Winde of Norfolk), ii. & iii. Or a chevron between three griffins' heads erased gules langued sable (Winde of Northumberland), 2nd and 3rd, Azure ten bezants, on a chief argent a lion passant sable ermined argent langued gules (Bridgman), impaling, Qly of 15, 1st and 15th, Gules a cross lozengy argent (Stawell), 2nd, Argent on a cross sable five

bezants (Stratton), 3rd, Sable a cross formy fitchy or (Columbers),
4th, Gules a bend or a label argent (Columbers), 5th, Azure ten
billets or (Gascelyn), 6th, Azure three bends argent (Merton), 7th,
Sable a chevron between three escallops argent (Faraway alias
Farewell), 8th, Argent a wyvern azure armed and langued gules
(   ), 9th, Gules a bend between six cross crosslets or (Preston),
10th, Vert a lion rampant or debruised by a bend argent (Beaupere),
11th, Gules a bend between six fusils or (   ), 12th, Argent two
chevrons gules a label azure (St Maur), 13th, Or a lion rampant within
an orle of cross crosslets azure (   ), 14th, Or a castle between
three battleaxes sable in chief a crescent gules (Hext)   Cherub's
head above   Motto: Virtus ubique quiescit
To dexter of main shield, on a lozenge, Or a chevron gules between
three lions' paws erect and erased sable armed gules, in chief the Badge
of Ulster (Austen), impaling Stawell A.Bl.   To sinister of main
shield, Qly, 1st and 4th, qly i. & iv. Winde of Norfolk, ii. & iii. Winde
of Northumberland, 2nd and 3rd, Bridgman, impaling, Stawell S.Bl.
Inscribed on back of hatchment: Elizabeth, Lady Austen, was 3rd
daughter of Col. George Stawell and Ursula Austen elder branch of the
Stawells of Somersetshire. The Atchievement was set up in Memory
of ye Lady Austen who died 18 Nov. 1725, by William Winde, Esq.
her Ladyship's 2nd husband, 1727.
(Hatchment is painted on metal)

BILSINGTON

1. Dexter background black
Argent a chevron sable between three moorhens proper (Luxmoore)
Crest: A moorhen proper   Mantling: Gules and argent, bearing on
the sinister side the seal of the Priory   Above and partly surrounding
the crest the initials A.F.C.C.L. in cursive characters   To dexter
and sinister of shield the dates 1876 and 1944
On the frame, counterchanged black and white, the lettering also
counterchanged: Sir Arthur Fairfax Charles Coryndon Luxmoore,
Knight, Lord Justice of Appeal, Privy Counsellor. A gift of affectionate
remembrance from the people of Bilsington and Bonnington.
For Sir Arthur Luxmoore, who d. 25 Sept. 1944.   (D.N.B.)

BIRLING

1. All black background
Qly, 1st and 4th, qly i. & iv. Gules on a saltire argent a rose gules
barbed and seeded proper (Nevill), ii. & iii. Or fretty gules on a canton

per pale ermine and or a lymphad sable pennons flying gules (Nevill),
2nd and 3rd, Gules three wolves' heads erased proper (Robinson)
Earl's coronet   Crests: Dexter, from a ducal coronet or a bull's head
proper armed or charged with a rose gules   Sinister, on a chapeau
gules and ermine a bull statant argent pied sable, collared and chain
reflexed over the back and at the end of the chain a staple or
Badges (below crests):   Dexter, A rose gules barbed and seeded
proper   Sinister, A portcullis or   Motto: Ne vile velis
Supporters: Two bulls argent pied sable, armed, unguled collared and
chained and at the end of each chain a staple or
For John, 3rd Earl of Abergavenny, in holy orders, who d. unm. 12
Apr. 1845.   (B.P. 1949 ed.)

2. Dexter background black
Qly, 1st and 4th, Nevill, as 1, 2nd and 3rd, Nevill, as 1, impaling, Qly,
1st and 4th, Argent on a chief gules a fleur-de-lys or over all a bend
engrailed azure (Leeke), 2nd and 3rd, Or on a bend gules three
crescents or (Otter)
Earl's coronet   Crest: As dexter of 1.   Badges, motto and
supporters: As 1.
For William 4th Earl of Abergavenny, in holy orders, who m. 1824,
Caroline, dau. of Ralph Leeke, of Longford Hall, Salop, and d.
17 Aug. 1868. She d. 19 May 1873.   (B.P. 1949 ed.)

BLACKHEATH, Morden College Chapel

1. Dexter background black
Argent a fleur-de-lys gules, the Badge of Ulster (Morden), impaling,
Azure two swords in saltire points upwards argent (Brand)
Crest: A lion rampant gules   Mantling: Gules and argent
Motto: In coelo salus   Skull in base
For Sir John Morden, Bt., who m. Susanna, dau. of Joseph Brand, of
Edwardstone, and d.s.p. 6 Sept. 1708.   (B.E.B.; Morden College)

2. All black background
On a lozenge
Arms: As 1.
For Susanna, widow of Sir John Morden, Bt., d. 27 June 1721.
(Sources, as 1; M.O.)

BOUGHTON ALUPH

1. Dexter background black
Qly, 1st and 4th, Azure a bend between six pierced molets or (Breton),

2nd and 3rd, Gules a mule statant a bordure argent (Moyle), impaling,
Argent on a bend gules a helm or (Trayton)
Crest: A lion's gamb couped erect or   Mantling: Azure and argent
Motto: Resurgam
Possibly for Moyle Breton, d. 1735.   (O.H.S.; Berry)

BOUGHTON MALHERBE

1. Sinister background black
Qly, 1st and 4th, Argent a human heart gules imperially crowned
proper, on a chief azure three pierced molets argent (Douglas), 2nd and
3rd, Sable a garb or a bordure argent (Stoddart), impaling, Argent
two bars wavy gules, on a chief gules a pierced molet of six points
argent (   )
Helm but no crest   Mantling: Gules and argent   Motto: Sapientia
et veritas
Unidentified

BOXLEY

1. Dexter background black
Per pale or and sable a pheon counterchanged (Whatman), impaling,
Azure on a mount in base vert a lamb passant or, on a chief argent
three bees volant proper (Gaussen)
Crest: A demi-lion rampant langued gules holding in his paws a pheon
or   Mantling: Gules and argent   Motto: Memento mori
For James Whatman, of Vintner's, who m. 1811, Eliza Susannah,
eldest dau. of Samuel Richard Gaussen, of Brookman's Park, Herts,
and d. 18 Sept. 1843.   (B.L.G. 5th ed.)

BREDGAR

1. All black background
Barry wavy of six argent and azure on a bend sable three boars' heads
couped or (Purcell), impaling, Per bend gules and or two leopards'
heads erased and counterchanged (Fearne)
Crest: A boar's head erased or langued gules   Mantling: Gules and
argent   Motto: Mors mihi lucrum
Unidentified

2. All black background
Fearne, impaling, Argent a chevron between three spearheads sable
(? Byland)
No helm or crest   Shield surround by gold decorative work and
surmounted by a skull   Motto: Mors janua vitæ
For James Fearne, who m. Elizabeth, dau. of Edmond Byland, and
d. Feb. 1709.   (M.I.)

CANTERBURY, Holy Cross, now Guildhall

1. All black background
Argent two bends engrailed sable (Staines)
Crest: A sinister arm vested per pale gules and azure holding an olive
branch proper   Mantling: Gules and argent   Motto: Resurgam
Two cherubs' heads at top corners of shield, and skull and crossbones
below
Probably for Richard Staines, Mayor of Canterbury in 1792, who d.
(N. E. Toke)

St Mildred

1. Sinister background black
Azure two lions combatant or langued gules (Carter), impaling, Gules a
fess chequy or and azure between ten billets four and six argent (Lee)
Mantling: Gules and argent   Motto: A posse ad esse
For Mary, dau. of Lancelot Lee of Cotton Hall, Salop, who m. as his
first wife, William Carter, M.D. of Canterbury, and d. 15 Sept. 1815.
(N. E. Toke; M.I.)

2. Dexter background black
Carter, impaling two coats per fess; in chief, Gules a fess chequy or
and azure between ten billets six and four azure (Lee), and in base, Or
on a chevron between three trefoils slipped sable three molets or
(Holworthy)
Crest: A lion's head erased or langued gules   Mantling: Gules and
argent   Motto: A posse ad . . .
For William Carter, M.D. of Canterbury, who m. 2nd, Sophia, dau. of
Henry Holworthy, of Ellesworth Hall, Cambridge, and d. 20 Sept.
1822, aged 37.   (N. E. Toke; M.I.)

3. Sinister background black
Argent a crossbow between four moorcocks sable, legged, crested and
jellopped gules (Highmore), impaling, Argent a mermaid gules, crined,

girdled and tailed or, holding in the dexter hand a mirror and in the
sinister a comb sable (Ellis)
On a mantle or and argent   Cherub's head above
For Anna Maria, dau. of the Rev. Seth Ellis, of Brampston, Derbyshire,
who m. Anthony Highmore, and d. Oct, 1794, aged 71.   (G.M.)

4. All black background
Qly, 1st and 4th, Highmore, 2nd and 3rd, Ellis as 3, but mirror and
comb or
Crest: A dexter arm embowed in armour proper brandishing fesswise
a falchion argent, hilt and pommel or, between two pikes gules, headed
or   Mantling: Gules and argent   Motto: Bello paratus paci intentus
Possibly for Anthony Highmore, son of 3, who d. 19 July 1829.   (G.M.)

5. All black background
On a lozenge   Highmore arms only
Above the lozenge are three cherubs' heads and below a skull
For Elizabeth Highmore, dau. of 3, who d. 1793, or her sister, Sarah,
who d. 23 Mar. 1814.   (N. E. Toke; G.M.)

6. All black background
Per fess vert and or a pale counterchanged and three trefoils slipped or
(Simmons)
Crest: An ermine courant in its summer coat, holding in its mouth a
trefoil slipped or   Mantling: Gules and argent   Motto: Vincit
qui patitur
Probably for Alderman James Simmons, who d. 22 Jan. 1807.   (M.I.)

St Stephen, Hackington

1. All black background
On a lozenge surmounted by a cherub's head
Argent two lions rampant gules supporting between them a tower sable
(Kelley)   Skull below
Possibly for Elizabeth Clarissa, dau. of Richard and Elizabeth Kelly,
who d. 21 Jan. 1880.   (M.I.)

(Two other hatchments at St Mildred's which bear inscriptions are
excluded, as are the three at St Alphege's, and the rectangular panels
at St Stephen's, Hackington; they will all be included in the final
volume, which will deal with transitional examples)

CHARLTON, nr Woolwich

1. Dexter background black
Qly, 1st and 4th, Argent on a chief indented gules three crosses formy

argent (Perceval), 2nd and 3rd, qly i. & iv. Barry nebuly of six gules
and or (Lovel), ii. & iii. Azure a lion rampant guardant between eight
fleurs-de-lys argent (Holland), impaling, Sable a wolf rampant and
in chief three estoiles or (Wilson)
Baron's coronet   Crest: A thistle proper   Motto: Sub cruce
candida   Supporters: Two griffins segreant azure, beaked, armed,
semy-de-lys, ducally gorged and chained or   All on a mantle gules
and ermine
For Charles George, 2nd Baron Arden, who m. 1787, Margaret Elizabeth
(d. 20 May 1851), eldest dau. of Gen. Sir Thomas Spencer Wilson, 6th
Bt., and d. 5 July 1840.   (B.P. 1965 ed.)

GREAT CHART

1. Sinister background black

Qly, 1st and 4th, Argent on a chevron between three greyhounds'
heads erased sable collared or three roundels argent (Toke
Augmentation), 2nd and 3rd, Per chevron sable and argent three
griffins' heads erased counterchanged langued gules (Toke)   In
pretence: Or a fess gules between three olive branches proper
(Roundell)
Mantling: Gules and argent
For Margaretta Eleanor, dau. and heir of William Roundell, of
Scrivenby, Knaresborough, Yorks, who m. 1762, John Toke, of
Godinton, and d. Mar. 1780.   (B.L.G. 1937 ed.; N. E. Toke)

2. All black background

Arms: As 1.
Crest: A griffin's head erased sable beaked and langued gules, holding
in his beak a sword argent pommel and hilt or   Mantling: Gules
and argent   Motto: In coelo quies
For John Toke, of Godinton, who d. 6 July 1819.   (Sources, as 1.)

3. Sinister background black

Qly, 1st, Toke Augmentation, 2nd, Toke, but griffins beaked or,
3rd, Sable a lion rampant ermine langued gules a chief or (Goldwell),
4th, Roundell, impaling, Qly, 1st, Sable a fess between three
battleaxes proper (Wrey), 2nd, Argent a cross engrailed gules between
four water-bougets sable (Bourchier), 3rd, qly i. & iv. Sable three
fleurs-de-lys or a bordure argent, for France, ii. & iii. England
(Plantagenet), 4th, Sable a bend argent cotised or between six lions
rampant or langued gules (Bohun)
Mantling: Gules and argent   Motto: Resurgam
For Anna Maria, dau. of Sir Bourchier Wrey, Bt. of Tawstock, Devon,
who m. 1791, Nicholas Roundell Toke, of Godinton, and d. 25 Feb.
1834.   (Sources, as 1.)

4. All black background

Qly, 1st, Toke Augmentation, 2nd, Toke, as 1, 3rd, Azure a chief or,
over all a lion rampant argent langued gules (Goldwell), 4th, Roundell,
impaling, Qly, 1st, Wrey, 2nd, Bourchier, 3rd, qly i. & iv. France,
ii. & iii. England (Plantagenet), iv. Azure a bend argent cotised or
between six lions rampant or (Bohun)
Crests: 1. A fox courant reguardant or   2. A griffin's head erased
per chevron sable and argent gutty sable, beaked or, langued gules,
in his beak a sword erect argent pommel and hilt gules   Mantling:
Gules and argent   Motto: Resurgam
For Nicholas Roundell Toke, of Godinton, who d. 19 Feb. 1837.
(Sources, as 1.)

5. Dexter background black

Qly, 1st and 4th, Toke, as 1, 2nd and 3rd, Toke Augmentation,
impaling, Argent a fess dancetty sable (West)
Crests: As 4, but in reverse order and blade of sword sable   Motto:
Militia mea multiplex
For the Rev. William Toke, of Godinton, who m. 1793, Sarah, dau. of
the Rev. Francis Marius West, D.D., and d. 2 May 1855.   (Sources, as 1.)

6. Dexter background black

Qly, 1st and 4th, Per chevron sable and argent three griffins' heads
erased counterchanged (Toke), 2nd and 3rd, Argent on a chevron
between three greyhounds' heads erased sable collared or three roundels
argent, on each collar three roundels sable (Toke Augmentation),
impaling, Qly, 1st and 4th, qly i. & iv. Argent on a fess gules three oval
buckles or in base three thistle leaves conjoined proper (Leslie), ii. &
iii. Argent on a bend azure three buckles or (Leslie), 2nd and 3rd,
Or a lion rampant gules langued argent, debruised by a bendlet sable
(Abernethy)
Crests: 1. A griffin's head erased per chevron sable and argent gutty
counterchanged, langued gules, in his beak a sword proper pommel and
hilt gules   2. A fox courant reguardant or   Mantling: Azure
and argent   Motto: Militia mea multiplex
For the Rev. Nicholas Toke, of Godinton, who m. 1837, Emma, 2nd
dau. of John Leslie, D.D., Bishop of Elphin, and d. 10 Apr. 1866.
(Sources, as 1.)

CHEVENING

1. All black background (should be dexter black)

Qly ermine and gules a crescent argent for difference (Stanhope),
impaling, Sable a fess chequy argent and azure between three
bezants (Pitt)

Earl's coronet   Crest: From a tower azure a demi-lion rampant or
langued and ducally crowned gules between the paws a grenade sable
fired or   Mantling: Gules and ermine   Motto: A Deo et rege
Supporters: Dexter, A talbot ermine   Sinister, A wolf or ducally
crowned gules   Each charged on the shoulder with a crescent
sable   Skull in base
For James, 1st Earl Stanhope, who m. 1714, Lucy, eldest dau. of
Thomas Pitt, of Boconnoc, Cornwall, and d. 5 Feb. 1720-1.
(B.P. 1949 ed.)

2. All black background
On a lozenge surmounted by a cherub's head
Stanhope, with a crescent sable for difference, impaling, Pitt
Countess's coronet   Motto and supporters: As 1.
For Lucy, widow of James, 1st Earl Stanhope, d. 24 Feb. 1723,
(B.P. 1949 ed.)

3. Dexter background black
Stanhope, as 2, impaling, Qly, 1st and 4th, Gules on a chevron between
three cinquefoils argent a buckle azure between two ermine spots, all
within a border or charged with eight thistles vert (Hamilton), 2nd and
3rd, Argent a fess wavy between three roses argent barbed proper
(Melrose)
Earl's coronet   Crest, mantling, motto and supporters: As 1.
Winged skull in base
For Philip, 2nd Earl Stanhope, who m. 1745, Grisel, dau. of Charles,
Lord Binning, and d. 7 Mar. 1786.   (B.P. 1949 ed.)

4. All black background
On a lozenge surmounted by a countess's coronet
Stanhope, no crescent, impaling, Qly, 1st and 4th, Hamilton, with four
ermine spots, 2nd and 3rd, Melrose, with roses gules barbed and seeded
proper
Motto: As 1.   Supporters: Dexter, as 1.   Sinister, A wolf or ducally
gorged azure   Each charged on the shoulder with a crescent azure
For Grisel, widow of Philip, 2nd Earl Stanhope, d. 28 Dec. 1811.
(B.P. 1949 ed.)

5. Sinister background black
Arms: As 2.
Viscountess's coronet   Motto: As 1.   Supporters: Dexter, As 1.
Sinister, A stag or plain collared and chained sable   Each charged
on the shoulder with a crescent sable
For Hester, dau. of William, 1st Earl of Chatham, who m. 1774, as his
1st wife, Charles, Viscount Stanhope (later 3rd Earl), and d. 20
July 1780.   (B.P. 1949 ed.)

6. All black background
On a lozenge   Stanhope, with a crescent azure for difference,
impaling, Vert on a cross argent five roundels gules (Grenville)
Countess's coronet   Mantle: Gules and ermine   Motto: As 1.
Supporters: Dexter, as 1.   Sinister, A wolf or langued gules ducally
crowned azure   Each charged on the shoulder with a crescent azure
For Louisa, dau. and sole heiress of the Hon. Henry Grenville, who
m. 1781, as his 2nd wife, Charles, Viscount Stanhope (later 3rd Earl),
and d. 6 Mar. 1829.   (B.P. 1949 ed.)

7. Sinister background black
Stanhope, as 2, impaling, Or a chevron cotised between three
demi-griffins the two in chief respectant sable langued gules (Smith)
Countess's coronet   Supporters: As 6, but crescents sable
For Catherine Lucy, 2nd dau. of Robert, 1st Baron Carrington, who m.
Philip Henry, 4th Earl Stanhope, and d. 1 Oct. 1843.
(B.P. 1949 ed.)

8. Sinister background black
Stanhope, as 4, impaling, Qly, 1st and 4th, Azure three molets within a
double tressure flory counterflory argent (Murray), 2nd and 3rd,
Gules three crosses formy argent (Barclay)
Motto: As 1.   Cherub's head above shield surrounded by gold
scrollwork
For Frederica Louisa, eldest dau. of David William, 3rd Earl of
Mansfield, who m. Col. the Hon. James Hamilton Stanhope, and d.
14 Sept. 1823.   (B.P. 1949 ed.)

9. All black background
On a lozenge surmounted by a cherub's head
Vert on a cross argent five roundels gules (Grenville), impaling, Sable
a cross between four fleurs-de-lys or (Banks)
Motto: Resurgam
For Margaret Eleanora, dau. of Joseph Banks, of Revesby Abbey,
who m. 1757, the Hon. Henry Grenville, and d. 19 June 1793.
(B.P. 1868 ed.)

10. Sinister background black
Qly, 1st and 4th, Gules two chevronels between three escallops argent
(Perkins), 2nd, Sable a chevron between three pickaxes argent
(Moseley), 3rd, Or a fess between three eagles displayed sable langued
gules (Moseley), impaling, Per chevron sable and argent three
elephants' heads erased counterchanged (Sanders)
Motto: Resurgam   Shield suspended from bow of green ribbon and
festoons and with a cherub's head at each top angle
For Susannah Sanders, who m. Frederick Perkins, of Chipstead Place,
and d. 7 Dec. 1851, aged 70. He d. 10 Oct. 1860, aged 80.   (M.I.)

CHIDDINGSTONE

1. All black background
On a lozenge surmounted by a cherub's head
Qly, 1st and 4th, Vairy argent and sable on a fess gules a crescent or
for difference (Bracebridge), 2nd and 3rd, Per pale indented argent and
sable (Bracebridge), impaling, Qly of six, 1st, Per fess gules and sable
three bezants (Streatfeild), 2nd, Gules a chevron between three
esquires' helms argent (Fremlyn), 3rd, Ermine on a pile gules a
leopard's face jessant-de-lys or (Terry), 4th, Argent a lion rampant
gules langued sable collared or (Ashdown), 5th, Ermine on a canton
azure a saltire or charged with five fleurs-de-lys gules (Beard), 6th, Or a
pheon and a bordure engrailed azure (Sidney)
Very wide frame covered with crape
For Harriet, dau. of Henry Streatfeild, who m. Walter Bracebridge and
d. 4 Mar. 1824.   (B.L.G. 1937 ed.)

2. Dexter background black
Qly, 1st and 4th, Argent on a fess between three crescents gules a
molet argent and in chief a label gules for difference (Ogle), 2nd and
3rd, Or an orle azure (Bertram), impaling, Qly, 1st and 4th, Vairy
argent and sable on a fess gules a crescent argent for difference
(Bracebridge), 2nd and 3rd, Per pale indented argent and sable
(Bracebridge)
Two crests: Dexter, An antelope's head erased proper armed or
Sinister, A bull's head couped azure ducally gorged gules armed or
Mantling: Gules and argent   Motto: Prenes en gre
For Henry Ogle, who m. Harriet Anne, dau. of Walter Bracebridge and
Harriet Streatfeild, and d. 17 Oct. 1841.   (Burke's Commoners, I, 273)

3. All black background
Argent on a fess engrailed between three escallops sable three eagles
displayed or (Reeve), impaling, Qly, 1st and 4th, Per fess gules and
sable three bezants (Streatfeild), 2nd and 3rd, Gules a chevron between
three esquires' helms argent (Fremlyn)
Crest: A squirrel with a nut proper   Mantling: Gules and argent
A small hatchment, c. 21 in. x 21 in.
Unidentified
(This hatchment, recorded in 1954, is now missing)

4. Dexter background black
Per fess gules and sable three bezants (Streatfeild), impaling, Argent a
lion rampant gules langued and armed sable collared purpure the
collar charged with three bezants (Ashdown)
Crest: An arm in armour proper, bent from the elbow, the forearm
encircled with a band tied in a knot gules, supporting a spear or with a
pennon showing argent a cross gules on the dexter side of the

spear, and gules three bezants fessways on the sinister; the pennon being turned round the spear to show part of both sides   Mantling: Gules and argent   Motto: Data fata sequutus   Skull in base
For Henry Streatfeild, of Chiddingstone, who m. 1665, Sarah, only dau. and heir of John Ashdown, of Hever, and d. 2 Mar. 1719.
(B.L.G. 1937 ed.)

5. Dexter background black
Qly of six, 1st and 6th, Streatfeild, 2nd, Gules a chevron between three esquires' helms argent garnished or (Fremlyn), 3rd, Ermine on a pile gules a leopard's face jessant-de-lys or (Terry), 4th, Argent a lion rampant gules collared or the collar charged with three bezants (Ashdown), 5th, Ermine on a canton sable a saltire gules thereon five fleurs-de-lys or (Beard)   In pretence: Or a pheon and a bordure engrailed azure (Sidney)
Crest, mantling and motto: As 4.   Winged skull in base
For Henry Streatfeild, of Chiddingstone, who m. 1752, Anne Sidney, natural daughter of Jocelyne, 7th Earl of Leicester, and d. 4 Apr. 1762.   (B.L.G. 1937 ed.)

6. Dexter background black
Streatfeild, with a crescent argent in fess point for difference, impaling to the dexter, Argent a fess between three crescents gules (Ogle), and to the sinister, Argent three weavers' shuttles sable tipped and with yarn and threads pendent or (Shuttleworth)
Crest: As 4, but with spear sable headed argent   Mantling and motto: As 4.
For Richard Thomas Streatfeild, of the Rocks and Copwood, Sussex, who m. 1st, Jane Esther, dau. of Admiral Sir Chaloner Ogle, Bt. She d.s.p. 1796. He m. 2nd, Anne, dau. of Robert Shuttleworth, of Barton Lodge, Lancs, and d. 26 Aug. 1813.   (B.L.G. 1937 ed.)

7. Dexter background black
Streatfeild, impaling to the dexter, Argent on a fess between three crescents gules a molet or (Ogle), and to the sinister, Sable a fess vairy or and argent between three cinquefoils argent (Scoones)
Crest: As 4, but band on arm or, and spear all argent   Mantling and motto: As 4.
For Henry Streatfeild, of Chiddingstone, who m. 1st, 1782, Elizabeth Catherine, dau. of the Very Rev. Newton Ogle, D.D., Dean of Winchester. She d. 24 June 1801. He m. 2nd, 1802, Charlotte, dau. of William Scoones, of Tonbridge, and d. 22 Aug. 1829.
(B.L.G. 1937 ed.)

8. Sinister background black
Streatfeild, impaling, Qly, 1st and 4th, Azure a cross hameçon argent

(Magens), 2nd and 3rd, Argent on a mount three trefoils issuant vert in chief a gem ring proper (Dorrien)
Motto: As 4. Shield surmounted by two cherubs' heads and surrounded with gilt scrollwork
For Maria, dau. of Magens Dorrien Magens, of Hammerdown Lodge, Sussex, who m. Henry Streatfeild, of Chiddingstone, and d. 1844.
(B.L.G. 1937 ed.)

9. All black background
Arms: As 8.
Crest: As 4, but band on arm or, and spear proper headed argent
Mantling and motto: As 4.
For Henry Streatfeild, who d. 16 July 1852.   (B.L.G. 1937 ed.)

10. Dexter background black
Qly, 1st and 4th, Streatfeild, 2nd and 3rd, Gules a chevron between three esquires' helms argent (Fremlyn), impaling, Ermine on a pile gules a leopard's face jessant-de-lys or (Terry)
Crest: As 4, but spear all argent   Mantling: Gules and argent
No motto, but on scroll: Neare this place lyeth ye Body of Rich. Streatfeild of this parish Gent qui obiit 15th Apr. Anno Dom. 1676 aged 65 yeares 4 months and 7 days   Frame decorated with skulls, crossbones and hourglasses
For Richard Streatfeild, of Chiddingstone, who m. 1636, Anne, dau. and coheir of William Terry, of Wadhurst, and d. 15 Apr. 1676.
(B.L.G. 1937 ed.; inscr. on hatchment)

CHILHAM

1. Dexter background black
Argent on a bend engrailed gules three Catherine wheels or, on a chief gules a crescent between two leopards' faces argent (Hardy), impaling, Gules three piles in point argent, on a chief or a roundel between two cross crosslets fitchy gules (Orr)
Crest: A dexter arm embowed in armour proper garnished or, the hand grasping a dragon's head erased fesswise the head to the sinister proper   Mantling: Gules and argent   Motto: Armé de foi hardi
For Charles Hardy, of Chilham Castle, who m. 1838, Catherine, dau. of James Orr, of Hollywood House, co. Down, and d. 16 Mar. 1867.
(B.P. 1939 ed.)

CHISLEHURST

1. All black background
Two oval shields   Dexter, Qly, 1st and 4th, Azure a chevron

between three escallops argent (Townshend), 2nd and 3rd, Qly gules
and or, in the first quarter a molet argent, and in fess point a
crescent argent for difference (Vere), impaling, Qly, 1st and 4th,
Argent three cinquefoils gules (Southwell), 2nd and 3rd, Chequy or
and azure a fess gules (Clifford)   Sinister, Qly, as dexter, impaling,
Argent three bends wavy sable, on a chief gules three bezants (Clements)
Viscount's coronet   Crest: A stag trippant, at gaze proper, charged
on the shoulder with a crescent argent   Mantling: Gules and ermine
Supporters: Dexter, A lion or, armed argent langued gules collared
and chained sable, charged on the shoulder with a pheon sable
Sinister, A stag sable, langued gules, attired or, collared and chained
or, charged on the shoulder with an escallop argent
For John Thomas, 2nd Viscount Sydney, who m. 1st, 1790, Sophia
Southwell, dau. of Edward, 20th Baron de Clifford, and 2nd, 1802,
Caroline (d. 9 Aug. 1805), dau. of Robert, 1st Earl of Leitrim, and d.
20 Jan. 1831.   (B.P. 1965 ed.)

2. All black background
Within the Order of Hanover and Badge of Order pendent below
Azure a chevron ermine between three escallops argent (Townshend)
Crest: A stag trippant sable   Mantling: Gules and argent   Two
flags on either side of shield
For Lt.-Col. Sir Horatio George Powys Townsend, K.C.H. Governor of
the Round Tower of Windsor Castle, who d. unm. 25 May 1843.
(B.P. 1965 ed.)

3. Dexter background black
Two oval shields   Dexter, within the Order of the Bath, Qly, 1st and
4th, Townshend, as 2, 2nd and 3rd, Vere   Sinister, Qly as dexter,
impaling, Sable on a cross engrailed between four eagles displayed
argent five lions passant guardant sable (Paget)
Earl's coronet   Crest: A stag trippant proper charged on the
shoulder with an escallop argent   Motto: Droit et avant
Supporters: Dexter, A lion or collared and chained sable charged on
the shoulder with a pheon azure   Sinister, A buck sable, attired,
collared and chained or charged on the shoulder with an escallop argent
For John Robert, 1st Earl Sydney, who m. 1832, Emily Caroline (d.
9 Mar. 1893), dau of Henry, 1st Marquess of Anglesey, K.G., and
d.s.p. 14 Feb. 1890.   (B.P. 1965 ed.)

CHISLET

1. Sinister background black
Qly, 1st and 4th, Or two flaunches gules each charged with a leopard's
head or (Denne), 2nd and 3rd, Argent a fess nebuly gules between

three lions rampant sable (Aylwin), impaling, Azure a chevron above
two bars or (Sprye)
Crest: A stag lodged or   Mantling: Gules and argent   Motto:
Vivit post funera virtus
For Jane Sprye, who m. John Denne, and d. 1800, aged 55. He d. 1813,
aged 64.   (Chislet Monuments, F. Haslewood)

2. Dexter background black
Qly, as 1, impaling, Qly gules and azure, on a bend ermine cotised or
three apples slipped and leaved proper (   )
Crest and mantling: As 1.   Motto: Fides in Deo
For George Denne, formerly of Chislet Court, late of the Paddock,
Canterbury, who d. 31 Mar. 1810, aged 34.   (M.I.)

3. All black background
On a lozenge surmounted by a cherub's head
Two coats per fess, in chief, Sable a stag trippant argent (Jones), in
base, Argent on a bend gules three lozenges argent (?Peart), impaling,
Ermine a fess dancetty sable (?Reynolds)
All on a mantle sable and argent
Possibly for Martha Reynolds, 2nd wife of Thomas Jones, d. 8
Oct. 1770.   (M.I.)

4. Sinister background black
Qly, 1st and 4th, Jones, 2nd, ?Peart, 3rd, Or a griffin segreant sable
langued gules within a bordure gules (Boys)
Helm, but no crest   Mantling: Gules and argent   No motto
Unidentified

CRANBROOK

1. All black background
Azure on a chevron argent three molets sable, in dexter chief the Badge
of Ulster (Roberts), impaling, Sable on a chevron or between three
griffins' heads erased argent langued gules three molets of six points
gules (Beale)
Crest: An eagle displayed argent langued and armed gules gorged with a
chaplet vert   Mantling: Gules and argent   Motto: Mors iter ad vitam
For Sir Thomas Roberts, 4th Bt., who m. 1683, Jane, dau. and co-heir
of Sir John Beale, Bt., of Farningham, Kent, and d. 20 Nov. 1706,
aged 47.   (B.E.B.)

2. Sinister background black
Roberts, with Badge of Ulster in dexter chief, impaling, and in
pretence, Qly, 1st and 4th, Or three bendlets azure a bordure gules

(Newbery), 2nd and 3rd, Or on a chief vert three martlets or (Watson)
Motto: Post funera virtus   Cherub's head above shield
For Elizabeth, dau. and co-heir of Samuel Newbery, of London, who
m. 1714, Sir Thomas Roberts, 5th Bt., and d. 30 July 1727.
(B.E.B.)

3. All black background
Qly of 12, 1st, Roberts, with Badge of Ulster, 2nd, Argent a cross
moline between four crescents gules, on a bend azure three bezants
(Tillye), 3rd, Azure on a mount vert a hart lodged argent within park pales
or (   ), 4th, Gules a bend raguly between two garbs or (Walworth),
5th, Sable a chevron engrailed argent between in chief two estoiles
argent and in base a garb or (Walworth), 6th, Argent a chevron per
chevron azure and gules between three dexter hands gules (Maynard),
7th, Gules a fess vair between three crosses formy or (Filley), 8th,
Gules fretty argent a canton ermine (Hewish), 9th, Argent a chevron
sable between three lions couchant gules (   ), 10th, Per pale
azure and gules three pheons or (Roberts), 11th, Argent two bars and
in chief three lions rampant sable (Howland), 12th, Sable on a chevron
or between three griffins' heads erased argent three estoiles gules
(Beale)
Crest: An eagle displayed argent gorged with a chaplet vert
Mantling: Gules and argent   Motto: Post funera virtus
For Sir Thomas Roberts, 5th Bt., who d.s.p. 5 Jan. 1729-30, or for Sir
Walter Roberts, 6th Bt., who d.s.p. 7 July 1745.   (B.E.B.)
(This hatchment was in poor condition when recorded in 1954, and
has since been destroyed)

4. All black background
Paly of six gules and sable three eagles displayed argent armed and
ducally crowned or (Cooke)   In pretence and impaling, Chequy or
and azure a bordure gules, on a canton argent a lion rampant gules
langued sable (Warren)
Crest: A demi-eagle per pale gules and sable ducally crowned or wingèd
argent   Mantling: Gules and argent   Motto: In coelo quies
For John Cooke of the Inner Temple, who m. — Warren, and d.
(Franks Cat. of Bookplates)

5. Sinister background black
Cooke, impaling, Argent three battleaxes, two and one, sable (   )
Motto: Post funera virtus   Shield surmounted by a skull and
surrounded by gilt scrollwork
Unidentified

6. All black background
Qly, 1st and 4th, Cooke, 2nd and 3rd, Chequy azure and or a bordure
gules on a canton argent a lion rampant gules (Warren), impaling, as 5.

Crest: A demi-eagle displayed per pale gules and sable armed and ducally crowned or langued gules winged argent   Mantling and motto: As 4.
Unidentified

7. Sinister background black
Cooke, impaling, Chequy argent and sable a chief gules (Palmer)
Motto: Viventes lugent   Shield surmounted by a skull and surrounded by gilt scrollwork
Unidentified

8. Sinister background black
Qly, 1st and 4th, qly France and England, 2nd, Scotland, 3rd, Ireland, over all a baton sinister gules charged with three roses barbed and seeded argent (Beauclerk)   In pretence: Azure on a chevron argent three molets sable (Roberts)
Duchess's coronet   Motto: Auspicium melioris aevi   Supporters: Dexter, An antelope argent armed or langued gules, collared gules the collar charged with three roses argent   Sinister, A greyhound argent, clawed gules, similarly collared   All on a mantle gules and ermine   Cherub's head above and skull below
For Jane, dau. and co-heir of Sir Walter Roberts, 6th Bt., of Glassenbury, who m. 1752, George, 3rd Duke of St Albans, and d. 16 Dec. 1778.   (B.P. 1949 ed.)

9. Sinister background black
Argent on a saltire engrailed sable five escallops or (Conolly), impaling, Gules a chevron between in chief three cinquefoils and in base a buglehorn or (Donkin)
Motto: On a shield surmounted by a cherub's head and surrounded by ornamental scrollwork
Unidentified

10. All black background
Arms: As 9, but buglehorn stringed or
Crest: A cubit arm in armour argent rimmed at the wrist or, the hand proper grasping an annulet or   Mantling: Gules and argent
Motto: Confido
Unidentified

11. Dexter background black
Ermine three cats passant guardant in pale argent (Adams), impaling, Argent a cross crosslet fitchy sable (Scott)
Crest: A greyhound's head erased argent langued gules   Mantling: Gules and sable   Motto: By faith and perseverance

For Thomas Adams, eldest son of Thomas Adams of Swifts Place, who
m. Frances, dau. of John Scott of Osbornes Lodge, and d. in Belgrave
Place, London, on 29 Aug. 1812, aged 39. She d. 19 Sept. 1849,
aged 77.   (M.I.)

CRUNDALE

1. All black background
Or two bars sable, on a chief sable three cinquefoils or, the Badge of
Ulster (Filmer), impaling, Argent a chevron between three hawks'
heads erased azure (Honywood)
Crest: On a tower or a falcon rising proper   Mantling: Gules and
argent   Motto: In coelo quies   Skull in base
For the Rev. Sir Edmund Filmer, 6th Bt., who m. 1756, Annabella
Christiana, eldest dau. of Sir John Honywood, Bt., and d. 27 June 1810.
(B.P. 1875 ed.)

DEAL, St George

1. All black background
Or five fusils conjoined in fess sable (Pennington), impaling, Sable a
cross moline or (   )
Crest: The sun in splendour proper   Mantling: Gules and or
Mottoes: (above crest) —h nimum credulus post—   (Below shield)
In coelo quies   Winged skull in base
For the Rev. Montague Pennington, who d. 15 Apr. 1849, aged 87.
His wife, Mary, d. 24 Mar. 1830, aged 67.   (M.I.)

St Leonard

1. All black background
Azure a chevron ermine between three griffins' heads erased argent
langued gules (Gardner)
Crest: A griffin sejant argent langued gules, resting its dexter claw on a
book sable garnished or   Mantling: Gules and argent   Winged
skull in base   A small hatchment, c. 2 ft. x 2 ft. excluding the wide
gold and black frame
Unidentified

2. Sinister background black
Sable ermined or a griffin segreant argent, legged, armed and langued or
(Baker)   In pretence: Sable fretty argent a lion rampant or (   )

Crest: From a naval coronet or a cubit mailed arm or holding a trident
fessways sable headed argent   Mantling: Gules and argent   Motto:
Manet post funera virtus
Unidentified

3. All black background
Baker   In pretence: Chequy azure and or a lion rampant argent
armed and langued gules (   )
Crest: As 2, but arm sable and trident gules headed or
Mantling: Gules and argent   Motto: In coelo quies
Unidentified

4. All brown background
Sable three chevronels ermine (Wise)
Crest: A demi-lion argent holding in the dexter paw a mace erect or
Mantling: Gules and argent   On motto scroll: In Memory of Mr.
Sampson Wise   A small hatchment, c. 2 ft. x 2 ft., including frame
For Sampson Wise, who d.

5. All black background
Azure a chevron argent between three standing bowls or, issuing
therefrom three boars' heads palewise argent tusked or langued gules
(Bowles)   To dexter of main shield, Sable three pheons argent
(Nicholls), impaling, Bowles D.Bl.   To sinister of main shield,
Argent a lion rampant within a bordure azure (Renton), impaling,
Bowles D.Bl.
No crest   Mantling: Gules and argent   On motto scroll: In
Memory of Mrs. Thomasin Renton   Frame decorated with skulls
and crossbones
For Thomasin Bowles, who m. 1st, George Nichols of Deal, and 2nd,
1710, Alexander Renton, and d.   (Mar. Lic.)

6. All brown background
Gules a chevron between three molets or (Poulton)
Crest: A lion's head erased affronté sable ducally gorged or
Mantling: Gules and argent
Frame decorated with skull and crossbones, and inscribed 'In Memory
of Capt. Tho: Poulton' and at top and base 16 and 99
For Capt. Thomas Poulton, who d. 1699.

7. All black background
Argent gutty gules a lion rampant sable crowned or (Scriven)
Helm, but no crest   Mantling: Gules and argent   On scroll
in position of crest: 'In Memory of M^{ris} Mary Screven who died ye
18th of Iune 1687 in ye 18th year of her age'   Frame decorated
with skulls and crossbones   A small hatchment c. 2 ft. 6 ins. x
2 ft. 6 ins.

8. All black background
Or a lion rampant gules within a bordure engrailed sable (Pomeroy),
impaling, Argent three roundels and a chief gules (Beesley)
Crest: A demi-lion gules in its dexter paw a bezant   Mantling:
Gules and argent   On broad scroll below shield: 'Here lieth the
body of Capt. George Pomeroy, son of Capt. Wm Pomeroy of the West
late Commander of their Majesties Ship the Rupert who received his
mortal wound against the French off Beachy and departed this life
the 25th day of July 1690 in ye 39th year of his age leaving his wife
and 3 children behind him.'
Frame decorated with skull and crossbones

9. All black background
Argent a saltire gules a label sable for difference (Gerard)
Crest: A monkey passant sable langued gules, collared and chained at
the waist or   Mantling: Gules and argent   On motto scroll:
In memory of Mr. Henry Gerard who departed this life the 27th of
September A° Dom. 1698 In ye 24th Yeare of his age'   Wide black
frame decorated with skulls, crossbones and monogram of HG

10. All black background
Argent a saltire gules a crescent sable for difference (Gerard)
Crest: A monkey passant sable collared at the waist and chained or
Mantling: Gules and argent   On motto scroll: 'In memory of
Mr. Henry Gerard late Rector of this Parish who departed this life the
2nd day of January in the 65th year of his age, Anno Dom. 1710'.
Frame decorated with skulls, crossbones and hourglasses

11. All brown background
Per chevron argent and sable in chief two fleurs-de-lys and in base a
tower or (Serocold)
Crest: A tower or surmounted by a fleur-de-lys argent   Mantling:
Gules and argent   Frame decorated with skulls and crossbones and
date 1705
Probably for George Serocold, buried at Deal, 23 Jan. 1705-6.
(Archaeologia Cantiana)

12. All brown background
Or a chevron sable between three choughs proper (   )
Crest (on a barred affronté helm); A chough rising proper
Mantling: Sable and or   A small hatchment with a wide frame
inscribed Obiit XX Martii at top and Anno MDCLXXXXVI at base
Unidentified

13. Dexter background black
Two oval shields   Dexter, within the Order of the Bath, Argent on
a chevron embattled gules between three bears' gambs erect erased sable

ermined argent three crescents or ermined sable (Harvey)   Sinister,
Harvey, impaling, Gules a chevron between three boars' heads couped
or (Bradley)
Crest: Two bears' gambs erect erased sable ermined argent holding a
crescent or ermined sable   Mantling: Gules and argent   Motto:
Servate fidem cineri
For Admiral Sir John Harvey, K.C.B., Admiral of the Blue, who m.
1797, Elizabeth, dau. of William Wyborn Bradley, of Sandwich, and d.
17 Feb. 1837.   (M.I.)
(This hatchment, when recorded in 1955, was in poor condition;
when checked in 1975 it was almost indecipherable)

14. All black background
Two oval shields   Dexter, within the Order of the Bath and with
star pendent below, Harvey, with a molet argent on a molet sable
for difference   Sinister, within an ornamental wreath, as dexter,
impaling, a blank
Crest, mantling and motto: As 13.   Supporters: Two sailors proper
in their exterior hands a staff with a flag argent charged with a cross
gules, in the dexter canton an anchor azure
For Admiral Sir Edward Harvey, G.C.B., who m. Eliza Ann (d. 23 Aug.
1857), only dau. of John Cannon, and d. 4 May 1865.   (M.I.)

15. Sinister background black
Sable a fess wavy between two estoiles of six points argent a molet or
for difference, the Badge of Ulster (Drake), impaling, vert a chevron
ermine between three griffins' heads erased or (? Hayman)
Motto: Sic parvis magna   Two cherubs' heads above shield
Presumably for Elizabeth Hayman, who m. as his 1st wife, Sir Francis
Samuel Drake, 1st and last Bt., and d. ? 1787.
(B.E.B.; Drake biography)
(This hatchment, when recorded in 1955, was in poor condition; when
checked in 1975 it was almost indecipherable)

16. All black background
Drake, as 15, impaling, Argent a fess gules between six choughs sable
(Onslow)
Crest: A sailing ship or, on a terrestrial globe, drawn by golden
hawsers, from a hand proper the arm habited gules cuffed argent issuing
from clouds proper   Mottoes: (above crest) Auxilio divino
(below shield) Sic parvis magna   Mantling: Gules and argent
For Sir Francis Samuel Drake, 1st and last Bt., who m. 2nd, Miss
Onslow, dau. of George Onslow, M.P., and d.s.p. 19 Nov. 1789.
(B.E.B.)

(Many of these hatchments bearing inscriptions, 'In Memory of . . .'
might appear to be memorials of a more permanent nature, and so not

qualify for inclusion; but there are so many that it seems they could
have been used as hatchments, but are a local variation from the norm.
No. 8 does not meet this condition, but is nevertheless included, as
it belongs to the same period as the other)

DODDINGTON

1. Dexter background black

Qly, 1st and 4th, Qly per fess indented or and gules in the first quarter
a lion passant guardant gules (Croft), 2nd and 3rd, Sable three weaving
combs argent (Tunstall), in centre point of 1st quarter the Badge of
Ulster, impaling, Argent two bends engrailed sable a canton gules
(Radcliffe)
Crest: A lion passant guardant per pale indented gules and or ermined
sable resting its dexter paw on an escutcheon charged with the Badge
of the Portuguese Order of the Tower and Sword   Over the crest the
motto: Valor e lealdade   Below the shield the motto: Esse quam
videri   Mantling: Gules and argent   Pendent below shield the
Badge of the same Portuguese Order   Supporters: Dexter, A lion
rampant guardant or gorged with a wreath of laurel proper, pendent
therefrom an escutcheon gules charged with a tower or   Sinister, A
bull sable, armed, unguled, ducally gorged and tip of tail or, langued
gules, charged on the shoulder with an escutcheon argent charged with
the Badge of the Order of the Tower and Sword
For Sir John Croft, 1st Bt., Knight Commander of the Royal
Portuguese Order of the Tower and Sword, who m. 1st, 1816, Amelia
Elizabeth (d. 20 Oct. 1819), dau. of James Warre, and 2nd, 1827,
Anne Knox, dau. of the Rev. John Radcliffe, and d. 5 Feb. 1862.
(B.P. 1875 ed.)
(The hatchment of Sir John's first wife is in the parish church at
Thornton Watlass, Yorkshire)

EASTRY

1. Background black behind dexter shield, lozenge and sinister side of sinister shield

A lozenge flanked by two shields   Dexter, An oval shield within
circlet of the Order of the Bath and laurel branches of Military
division, Argent on a fess azure between two cotises engrailed sable
three crescents argent, in centre chief an anchor sable supported by
two lions rampant respectant gules, on a canton gules the Badge of the
Sicilian Order of St Ferdinand of Merit (Staines)   On lozenge,
Staines, with in pretence, Qly, 1st and 4th, Or on a pale gules a sword

erect argent pommel and hilt or, on a chief azure three bezants
(Bargrave), 2nd and 3rd, Argent a chevron between three oxen statant
sable (Tournay)   Sinister shield, Gules on a fess between three
doves argent three crosses formy gules, in chief a medal argent stringed
sable (Gunning)   In pretence: Qly, 1st and 4th, Bargrave, 2nd and
3rd, Tournay
Three medals pendent between dexter shield and lozenge   Lozenge
surmounted by two cherubs' heads
For Sarah, dau. of Robert Tournay Bargrave, of Eastry Court, who
m. 2nd, 1819, Sir Thomas Staines, K.C.B. He d. 13 July 1830. She m.
3rd, George Gunning, and d. 25 Jan. 1832.
(D.N.B.; M.I. in Margate church)
(There is another hatchment for Sarah Gunning in Margate parish church,
and also the hatchment of her second husband, Sir Thomas Staines)

2. All black background
Qly, 1st and 4th, Bargrave, 2nd and 3rd, Tournay   In pretence:
Qly, 1st and 4th, Argent three trees vert (   ), 2nd and 3rd, Bargrave
Crests: Dexter, On a mound vert a pheon gules between two laurel
branches vert   Sinister, A bull's head erased argent, armed or, with
a collar azure charged with three bezants   Mantling: Gules and
argent   Motto: In coelo quies   Skull in base
For Robert Tournay Bargrave, who m. Christiana, dau. of Claudius
Clare, by Christiana, dau. and heiress of Isaac Bargrave of Eastry
Court, and d. 19 May 1825.   (Berry)

FORDCOMBE

1. Dexter background black
A shield and a cartouche   Dexter, within motto of Bath and Badge
of Order pendent below, Gules on a chevron argent fimbriated or
three escallops sable (Hardinge)   Sinister, Hardinge, impaling, Qly,
1st and 4th, Or a bend countercompony argent and azure between
two lions rampant gules (Stewart), 2nd and 3rd, Gules a saltire argent
(Nevill)
Viscount's coronet   Crest: A mitre gules, each point surmounted by
a cross formy or, thereon a chevron argent cotised or charged with
three escallops sable   Motto: Mens aequea rebus in arduis
Supporters: Dexter, A lion rampant proper murally crowned or
Sinister, A lion rampant proper crowned with an Eastern crown or
Each supporter with a flagstaff proper bearing a flag or, the flags
flowing to dexter and sinister respectively
For Henry, 1st Viscount Hardinge, G.C.B., who m. 1821, Emily Jane
(d. 18 Oct. 1865), dau. of Robert, 1st Marquess of Londonderry, and d.
24 Sept. 1856.   (B.P. 1949 ed.)

2. Sinister background black
Gules on a chevron argent cotised or three escallops sable (Hardinge),
impaling, Sable a bend cotised between six crosses formy or (Bingham)
Viscountess's coronet   Supporters: As 1.
For Lavinia, dau. of George, 3rd Earl of Lucan, who m. 1856, Charles
Stewart, 2nd Viscount Hardinge, and d. 15 Sept. 1864.   (B.P. 1949 ed.)

FORDWICH

1. All black background
Gules a chevron between three griffins' heads erased argent langued
sable, on a chief argent a lion passant gules between two annulets
gules (Jennings)
Crest: A cat's head erased or semy of roundels sable holding in its
mouth a cross formy fitchy or   Mantling: Gules and argent
Skull and crossbones below
For Anthony Jennings, who d. 15 May 1830, aged 73.   (M.I.)

2. All black background
Qly of 12, 1st, Gules a cross potent ermine (Norton), 2nd, Gules a
cross crosslet ermine (Norton), 3rd, Gules an eagle displayed argent
(Atbridge), 4th, Ermine a fess engrailed gules (Quadring), 5th, Sable a
fess between three leverets or (Leverett), 6th, Sable two bars or a chief
argent (Frognall), 7th, Sable a cross voided or (Apuldrefield), 8th,
Ermine a fess vairy or and gules (Apuldrefield), 9th, Ermine on a bend
azure three lions rampant or (Bourne), 10th, Argent on a chevron
gules three talbots or (Martyn), 11th, Sable three bars or an
inescutcheon gules, on a chief or two pales sable (Beverley), 12th,
Azure on a chevron between three lozenges or a trefoil slipped azure
(Hide), impaling, Argent two chevronels sable between three roses
gules barbed and seeded proper (Wickham)
Crest: A wolf's head erased or langued gules charged on the neck with
a crescent argent   Mantling: Gules and argent
For Valentine Norton, who m. Katherine, only dau. and heir of
William Wickham, and d. 1650.   (Fane Lambarde)

3. All black background
Qly of 12, 1st, Azure a lion rampant or langued and crowned gules, in
chief a crescent argent for difference (Darrell), 2nd, Argent a fess
dancetty gules in chief three molets sable (Barrett), 3rd, Or a saltire
sable (Dering), 4th, Or a cross engrailed gules in centre point a crescent
argent (Haute), 5th, Gules a cross crosslet ermine (Norton), 6th, Gules
an eagle displayed argent (Atbridge), 7th, Argent a bend gules between
two cotises nebuly sable (Surrenden), 8th, Or a fleur-de-lys sable
(Pluckley), 9th, Sable three buglehorns stringed argent (Horne), 10th,

Azure a fess or in chief two cross crosslets fitchy or (   ), 11th,
Argent a cross engrailed between four bears' heads erased sable
(Bettenham), 12th, Gules a wyvern displayed argent (Brent), impaling,
Per pale ermine and or a tower triple-towered sable (Hooper)
Crest: From a ducal coronet or a Saracen's head couped at the
shoulders proper on the head a cap azure fretty and tasselled or
Mantling: Gules and argent
For Robert Darrell, who m. 2nd, Elizabeth, dau. of John Hooper, and
d. 1668.
(Fane Lambarde; Fordwich, the Lost Port)

GROOMBRIDGE

1. Dexter background black

Argent a fess countercompony or and gules in chief three cross crosslets
gules (Burges), impaling, Argent a fess ermine between three martlets
sable (   )
Crest: A stag trippant proper   Mantling: Gules and argent
Motto: Resurgam
For Robert Burges, who m. Sarah, and d. 29 Jan. 1794, aged 64.   (M.I.)

2. Dexter background black

Argent a chevron between three roundels gules (? Harbroe), impaling,
Argent a fess ermine between three martlets sable (   )
Crest: An increscent argent   Mantling: Gules and argent
Motto: Resurgam
For James Harbroe, who m. Sarah, widow of Robert Burges, and d.
20 Feb. 1802, aged 66. She d. 22 June 1841, aged 79.   (M.I.)

HADLOW

1. Dexter background black

Sable a stag's head erased argent langued gules attired or holding in the
mouth a molet or, within a bordure or charged with three escallops
sable (Rodger), impaling, Qly, 1st and 4th, Sable three conies courant
argent (Cunliffe), 2nd and 3rd, Argent three eagles wings elevated
sable, on a chief gules three fountains (Pickersgill)
Crest: On a mount a stag salient between two laurel branches proper
Mantling: Sable and argent   Motto: Nos nostraque deo
For Robert Rodger, of Hadlow Castle, who m. 1844, Sophia, eldest
dau. of John Pickersgill and Sophia Cunliffe, and d. 17 Aug. 1882.
(B.L.G. 7th ed.)

2. All black background

Qly, 1st and 4th, Or on a bend gules three cross crosslets or (Polhill), 2nd and 3rd, Vert an eagle displayed or (Buckland), impaling, Qly, 1st and 4th, Ermine on a fess gules three annulets or (Barton), 2nd and 3rd, Argent two lions combatant gules langued sable (Lucas)
Crest: From a mural coronet or a hind's head proper between two oak branches vert fructed or   Motto: In coelo quies
Probably for the Rev. John Bosanquet Polhill, of Addington, who m. Elizabeth, dau. of Walter Barton (who later assumed the name of May) and was bur. 25 Feb. 1825.   (Misc. Gen. et Her., N.S. 3)

3. Sinister background black

Ermine on a fess gules three annulets argent (Barton), impaling, Or two chevrons and a canton gules (Kirrill)
Crest: A boar's head argent, langued gules, armed or   Mantling: Gules and argent
For Frances, dau. of Thomas Kirrell of Hadlow, who m. Henry Barton of Folkestone, and d. 1714.   (Sources, as 2.)

4. All black background

Qly of six, 1st, Gules a fess between eight billets or (May), 2nd, Barton, as 3, 3rd, Argent a tower between three keys wards upwards sable (Baker), 4th, Argent two lions combatant gules in centre chief a crescent sable (Lucas), 5th, Argent a fess between eight keys wards downwards sable (   ), 6th, Or a chevron gules between three greyhounds courant argent (Gainsford)
Crest: From a ducal coronet or a leopard's head proper langued gules
Mantling: Gules and argent   Motto: In coelo quies
Possibly for John, son of John Barton and Jane (née May), d. 1809. (Source, as 2.)

5. All black background

Qly, 1st and 6th, May, 2nd, Barton, as 3, 3rd, Or a chevron gules between three greyhounds courant sable (Gainsford), 4th, Lucas, 5th, Baker, impaling, Sable three bells argent a canton ermine (Porter)
Crest: From a ducal coronet or a leopard's head proper langued gules
Mantling: Gules and or   Motto: Nil desperandum
For Walter Barton-May, who m. 1822, Mary Susannah, dau. of John Porter, of Fish Hall, Kent, and d. 31 May 1855.   (M.I.)

6. All black background

Qly, 1st and 4th, Vert a dolphin naiant tail erect or (Monypenny), 2nd, Azure three cross crosslets fitchy issuing from as many crescents argent (Cathcart), 3rd, Paly of six argent and azure on a chief gules a lion passant guardant or all within a bordure ermine (Blackwell), impaling, Qly, 1st and 4th, Argent a fess azure in chief three roundels gules (Dering), 2nd and 3rd, Or a saltire sable (Dering)

Crest: Neptune bestriding a dolphin naiant in the sea, in his dexter hand the reins, in his sinister his trident, all proper   Mantling: Or
Motto: Temperat aequor
For the Rev. Phillip Monypenny, Vicar of Hadlow, who m. 1803, Charlotte, dau. of Sir Edward Dering, 6th Bt., and d. 1841. She d. 1836.   (B.P. 1939 ed.)

7. Dexter background black
Argent two bars and in chief three ? eagles' heads couped sable a canton gules (   ), impaling, Or a bear sejant and muzzled sable collared and chained or (   )
Crest: Sable a demi-? eagle wings erect argent   Mantling: Gules and argent   Motto: . lloeso lumine solem
Unidentified

UPPER HARDRES

All the following seven hatchments were recorded in 1955, but have since been destroyed.

1. Dexter background black
Gules a lion rampant ermine in dexter chief the Badge of Ulster (Hardres), impaling, Argent on a chevron sable between three rooks proper three chess rooks argent (Rooke)
Crest: A stag's head couped or   Mantling: Gules and argent
For Sir Thomas Hardres, 3rd Bt., who m. Ursula, dau. of Sir William Rooke, and d. 23 Feb. 1688.   (B.E.B.)

2. Dexter background black
Gules a lion rampant ermine over all a chevron or, in dexter chief the Badge of Ulster (Hardres), impaling, Argent a fess dancetty between three Cornish choughs proper (Thomas)
Crest: A stag's head couped or attired gules and azure   Mantling: Gules and argent   Motto: In silentio fortitudo
For Sir William Hardres, 4th Bt., who m. Elizabeth, dau. of Richard Thomas of Lamberhurst, and d. 8 July 1736.   (B.E.B.)

3. All black background
On a lozenge
Arms: As 2.
No motto   All on a mantle gules and argent
For Elizabeth, widow of Sir William Hardres, 4th Bt., bur. 22 June 1755.   (G.E.C.)

4. All black background
On a lozenge surmounted by a cherub's head

Hardres, as 2;　　In pretence: Or two ravens sable within an orle
engrailed gules charged with 12 bezants (Corbett)　　Skull below
For Frances, dau. and co-heir of John Corbet of Bourn Place, who m.
Sir William Hardres, 5th Bt., and d. 23 Feb. 1783.　　(B.E.B.; M.O.)

5. All black background
On a lozenge
Gules a lion rampant ermine (Hardres)
Motto: In coelo quies
Possibly for Anne, dau. of Sir Richard Hardres, 1st Bt., who d. 1680.
(Arch. Cant. Vol. IV)

6. Sinister background black
Argent a lion rampant vert (Jones), impaling, Argent a bend plain
cotised engrailed sable (Whitfield)
Crest: A sun in splendour or　　Mantling: Gules and argent
For Roberta Whitfield, who m. as his 1st wife, the Rev. David Jones,
Rector of Upper Hardres, and d. 23 Oct. 1744.　　(P.R.; M.O.)

7. Dexter background black
Three coats per pale　　1. Argent a lion rampant vert (Jones),
2. Argent a bend plain cotised engrailed sable (Whitfield), 3. Gules a lion
rampant ermine over all a chevron or (Hardres)
Crest and helm torn away　　Mantling: Gules and argent
For the Rev. David Jones, Rector of Upper Hardres, who m. 1st,
Roberta Whitfield, and 2nd, Elizabeth Hardres, and d. 20 Aug. 1750.
(P.R.; M.O.)

HARTLIP

1. All black background
Qly, 1st and 4th, Argent on a bend sable three pheons or, in chief a
molet sable (Bland), 2nd and 3rd, Qly azure and argent, on a cross or
five annulets gules, in second and third quarters an ermine spot
(Osborne), impaling, Or a lion rampant sable debruised by a bend
compony argent and gules (Faussett)
Crest: A lion's head erased argent issuing from a ducal coronet or
Mantling: Gules and argent　　No motto　　Urn in base
For William Bland, who m. Elizabeth Faussett, and d. 1835. She
d. 1789.　　(O.H.S.)

HOLLINGBOURNE

1. Dexter background black
Azure a lion's paw in fess erased between two lengths of chain or

(Duppa)   In pretence: Argent a sword erect in pale argent pommel and
hilt or entwined with two snakes and transfixing a heart gules (?Baas)
Crest: A dexter arm embowed in armour grasping a lion's paw erased
in fess or   Mantling: Gules and argent   Motto: Resurgam
Possibly for the Rev. Richard Hancorn, who assumed the name and
arms of Duppa. He m. a Miss Baas of Germany, an heiress, and d. 1790.
(B.L.G. 2nd ed.)

2. All black background
Duppa, impaling, Ermine a chief azure over all a bend gules charged
with a sword argent hilt and pommel or (Gladwyn)
Crest: A dexter arm embowed in armour proper garnished at the elbow
or grasping a lion's paw erased in fess or   Mantling and motto: As 1.
Cherubs' heads at top corners of shield and skull in base
For Baldwin Duppa Duppa, of Hollingbourne, who m. 1800, Mary,
dau. of Major-General Gladwin, of Stubbing Court, Derbyshire, and d.
5 Apr. 1847.   (B.L.G. 1937 ed.)

HORTON KIRBY

1. All black background
On a lozenge surmounted by a cherub's head
Gules a bend between ten cross crosslets or (Hornsby), impaling, Argent
three pallets gules a bordure engrailed azure, on a canton gules a spur
rowel downwards or (Knight)
Motto: Tempus edax rerum   Skull in base
For Elizabeth (Knight) who m. Richard Hornsby of Kirby Court, and
was bur. 1 Dec. 1791, aged 61. He d. 1772, aged 65.   (M.I.)

IGHTHAM

1. Dexter background black
Azure a griffin passant or armed and langued gules a chief or (Evelyn)
In pretence: Evelyn
Crest: A griffin passant or, beaked, forelegged and ducally gorged
azure, taloned and langued gules   Mantling: Gules and argent
Motto: Resurgam
For Alexander Hume, who took the name and arms of Evelyn. He m.
Frances Evelyn, and d. Feb. 1837.   (Toke M.S.)

2. All black background
On a lozenge surmounted by a cherub's head
Arms: As 1.   Mantling: Gules and argent
For Frances, widow of Alexander Evelyn. She d. Mar. 1837.
(Sources, as 1.)

3. Dexter background black
Argent two bars embattled counterembattled gules (James), impaling,
Azure a chevron between three lions' heads erased or langued gules
(Wyndham)
Crest: From a ducal coronet or a demi-swan rising proper
Mantling: Gules and argent   Motto: Mors janua vitæ
For William James, of Ightham Court, who m. Anne, only dau. and
heir of Sir Thomas Wyndham, Bt., of Trent, Somerset, and was bur.
12 Sept. 1718.   (B.L.G. 5th ed.; P.R.)

4. Dexter background black
Two shields, one slightly overlapping the other, each bearing the arms
of James
Crest and mantling: As 3.   Motto: In coelo quies   Skull in base
For William James, of Ightham Court, who m. Elizabeth, dau. of
Demetrius James, of Reigate, and was bur. 24 Dec. 1781.
(Sources, as 3.)

5. All black background
On a lozenge surmounted by a cherub's head
Arms: As 4, but wife's coat in pretence   Mantling: Gules and argent
Motto: Resurgam
For Elizabeth, widow of William James. She was bur. 23 Nov. 1798.
(Sources, as 3.)

6. Dexter background black
Qly, 1st and 4th, James, 2nd, Argent a chevron between three millrinds
azure (James), 3rd, Argent three bars wavy azure on a chief or three
falcons rising proper (Moriskins), impaling, Azure a lion rampant
guardant between three escallops argent (Gibbons)
Crest: From a ducal coronet argent a swan rising proper beaked or
Mantling and motto: As 5.
Probably for Col. Richard James, of Ightham Court, son of William
and Elizabeth James, who m. Letitia Gibbons, and d.s.p. Nov. 1817.
(Sources, as 3.)

7. All black background
Qly, 1st and 4th, James, 2nd and 3rd, Argent on a fess between three
roundels azure each charged with a lion's head erased argent a griffin
passant between two escallops or (Grevis)
Crests: Dexter, from a ducal coronet or a swan rising proper beaked or
Sinister, A grey squirrel sejant proper in its paws an escallop or
Mantling: Gules and argent   Motto: Fide et constantia
Probably for Demetrius Grevis-James, of Ightham Court, son of Charles
Grevis and Elizabeth James, who m. 1812, Mary, dau. of James Shutt,
and d. 5 Aug. 1861; or his son, Demetrius Wyndham Grevis-James, who
d. unm. 10 Dec. 1901.   (B.L.G. 5th.; Misc. Gen. et Her. V.)

8. Dexter background black
Qly, 1st and 4th, Argent a chevron between three cocks gules (Cobb),
2nd and 3rd, Argent a chevron gules between three bulls' heads
cabossed sable (Curteis), impaling, Gules on a fess or between three
boars' heads couped argent langued azure two lions passant sable
langued gules (Wyatt)
Crest: From a ducal coronet or a demi-leopard argent spotted sable
langued gules   Mantling: Gules and argent   Motto: Fuimus
For the Rev. Thomas Cobb, Rector of Ightham, who m. Miss Wyatt, of
Chelsea, and d. 26 Nov. 1817.   (G.M.)

9. Dexter background black
Qly, 1st and 4th, Argent a chevron engrailed between three crabs claws
towards the dexter gules (Bythesea), 2nd and 3rd, Azure a bend or
on a chief argent two choughs proper (Vyner), impaling, Gules three
garbs or within a bordure engrailed or charged with eight roundels
vert (Kemp)
Crest: An eagle displayed or langued gules   Mantling: Gules and
argent   Motto: Mors janua vitæ   Cherub's head above and
skull in base
For the Rev. George Bythesea, Rector of Ightham, who m. Anne, dau.
of Thomas Reed Kemp, of Lewes Castle, Sussex, and d. Dec. 1800.
(N. E. Toke)

10. All black background
Azure a dexter hand apaumy couped at the wrist argent (Brome),
impaling, Bythesea
Crest: A cubit arm erect vested gules cuffed argent holding in the hand
a slip of broom proper   Mantling: Gules and argent   Motto: Resurgam
For Charles Brome, of West Malling, who m. Cecilia, dau. of William
Bythesea, of Greenwich, and d. 26 Apr. 1830.
(N. E. Toke; G.M.)

11. Dexter background black
Barry of ten or and azure (Selby), impaling, Argent a fess and in chief a
lion passant guardant gules (Walford)
Crest: A Saracen's head and shoulders, affronté proper, wreathed at the
temples azure and or   Mantling: Gules and argent   Motto: Fort
et loyal
For Thomas Selby, of Ightham Mote, who m. Elizabeth, dau. of Robert
Walford, of Whitley, Essex, and d. 5 Mar. 1820.   (N. E. Toke; G.M.)

12. All black background
Sable a chevron between three fleurs-de-lys argent (Howell)
Crest: From a ducal coronet or a buck's head erased argent
Mantling: Gules and argent   Motto: In morte quies
Unidentified

IGHTHAM Mote

1. Dexter background black
Three coats per pale   1. Argent two beavers facing sinister proper
(Somes), 2. Ermine a cinquefoil gules, on a canton azure a buglehorn
stringed or (Dover), 3. Per bend argent and or on a bend engrailed
sable between two sinister wings elevated gules another bend plain
counterchanged charged with three garlands of roses gules (Saxton)
No helm or mantling   Crest: On a castle tripletowered argent a
cockatrice affronté vert combed and wattled gules wings expanded
proper   Motto: Do ever good   Supporters: Dexter, A talbot
argent   Sinister, A horse argent
c. 18 ins. x 18 ins.   Painted on silk
Inscription on frame: Used at the funeral of Joseph Somes, Esq. at
Stepney Church, July 2nd, 1845.

KENNINGTON

1. Dexter background black
Azure two lions combatant or (Carter)   In pretence: Qly, 1st and
4th, Argent a chevron between in chief two pierced molets and in
base an annulet sable (Plumptre), 2nd, Argent on a saltire sable five
fleurs-de-lys or (Hawkins), 3rd, Or a cross engrailed gules (   )
Crest: A lion's head erased or   Mantling: Gules and argent
Motto: A posse ad esse
For Harry William Carter, of Kennington Hall, who m. 1822, Louisa,
4th dau. of the Rev. Henry Plumptre, of Paulton, Somerset, and d. 16
July 1863.   (B.L.G. 1937 ed.)

2. All black background
Carter arms only
Crest and mantling: As 1.   Motto: Mors janua vitæ
Possibly for George William Carter, who d. unm. 1898.   (Source, as 1)

KINGSTON

1. Dexter background black
Qly, 1st and 4th, Azure a lion rampant argent (Byrch), 2nd and 3rd,
Azure on a chevron argent between three fleurs-de-lys or a cross clechy
gules, on a chief gules a portcullis argent (Byrch), impaling, Qly, 1st and
4th, Or on a chevron between three molets sable three lions passant
guardant or (Barrett), 2nd and 3rd, Or three roses gules barbed and
seeded proper (Barrett)

Crest: A eagle rising proper in its dexter claw a staff ending in a
fleur-de-lys or with a banner sable bearing a cross as in the arms or
Mantling: Gules and argent   Motto: In coelo quies
For the Rev. W. Dejoras Byrche, who m. Elizabeth, sister to Thomas
Barrett of Lee Priory, and d.   (Fane Lambarde)
(This hatchment was in poor condition when recorded in 1955, and
is now missing)

KNOLE HOUSE

1. All black background
Two lozenges   Dexter, surmounted by a countess's coronet, Argent
a bend sable in sinister chief a garb gules (Whitworth)   In pretence:
Argent on a chevron azure between three roses gules barbed and
slipped vert three fleurs-de-lys or (Cope)   Supporters: Two eagles
wings elevated sable langued gules beaked and membered or, each
ducally gorged or pendent therefrom an escutcheon argent charged with
a garb gules   Sinister, surmounted by a duchess's coronet, Qly
argent and gules over all a bend vair (Sackville)   In pretence: Cope
Supporters: Two leopards proper langued gules   All on a mantle
gules and ermine
For Arabella Diana, eldest dau. and co-heir of Sir Charles Cope, Bt., of
Brewerne, who m. 1st, John Frederick, 3rd Duke of Dorset, and 2nd,
Charles, Earl Whitworth, and d. 1 Aug. 1825, aged 58.
(B.P. 1949 ed.; B.E.P.; M.I. in Withyham church)
(There is an identical hatchment in the parish church at Withyham,
Sussex)

2. All black background
Qly or and gules over all a bend vair (Sackville)
Duke's coronet   Crest: From a coronet of fleurs-de-lys or an
estoile of eight points argent   Motto: Aut nun quam tentes aut
perfice   Supporters: Two leopards argent langued gules spotted
sable   All on a mantle gules and ermine
For Charles, 2nd Duke of Dorset, who d.s.p. 6 Jan. 1769, or for George
John Frederick, 4th Duke of Dorset, who d. unm. 14 Feb. 1815.
(B.P. 1949 ed.)
(There is an identical hatchment in the parish church at Withyham,
Sussex)

3. All black background
Qly of six, qly i. & iv. Argent a fess dancetty sable (West), ii. & iii.
Qly or and gules a bend vair in centre chief a cross crosslet
counterchanged (Sackville), 2nd, Azure three leopards' faces
jessant-de-lys or (Cantilupe), 3rd, Gules a lion rampant within eight
cross crosslets fitchy argent (De La Warr), 4th, Azure two bars gemel

and in chief a lion passant guardant or (Tregoz), 5th, Argent a fess
gules between three molets of six points sable (Ewyas), 6th, Gules three
bendlets or (Gresley)   In pretence: Qly or and gules over all a bend
vair (Sackville)
On a lozenge surmounted by a countess's coronet
Supporters: Dexter, A wolf cowed argent langued gules gorged with
a plain collar or   Sinister, A cockatrice or winged azure
For Elizabeth, Baroness Buckhurst, dau. and co-heir of John Frederick,
3rd Duke of Dorset, who m. 1813, George John, 5th Earl De La Warr,
and d. Jan. 1870.   (B.P. 1949 ed.)
(Husband's hatchment is at Withyham, Sussex)

4. Dexter background black

Two oval shields   Dexter, within the Order of Hanover, Qly, 1st and
4th, Gules three tilting spears or headed argent two and one (Amherst),
2nd, Argent on a fess azure three crosses formy or (Kirby), 3rd, Or
two pales gules on a chief gules three escallops or (   )
Sinister, within an ornamental band, as dexter, with in pretence, Qly or
and gules over all a bend vair (Sackville)   Badge of Order pendent
from a ribbon azure between the two shields
Earl's coronet   Crest: On a mount vert three tilting spears points
upwards or headed argent, one in pale and two in saltire entwined by a
laurel wreath proper   Motto: Constantia et virtute   Supporters:
Two Canadian War Indians of a copper colour, rings in nose, ears and
bracelets on arms and wrists argent, over shoulders two buff belts in
saltire, suspended from one a powder horn from the other a scalping
knife proper, their waists covered by a short apron azure fimbriated or,
gaiters edged or and shoes azure, ankles fettered together and fastened
by a chain or to the bracelet of the outer wrist; the dexter Indian
holding in his exterior hand an axe proper, the sinister Indian holding
in his exterior hand a tomahawk, thereon a scalp proper
For William, 1st Earl Amherst, who m. 2nd, Mary, dau. and co-heir of
John Frederick, 3rd Duke of Dorset, and d. 13 Mar. 1857.
(B.P. 1949 ed.)

5. All black background

Two shields   Dexter, within the Order of Hanover, Gules three
tilting spears or headed argent two and one (Amherst)   Sinister, as
dexter, with in pretence, Qly argent and gules over all a bend vair
(Sackville)
Countess's coronet   Supporters: As 4.
For Mary, dau. and co-heir of John Frederick, 3rd Duke of Dorset, who
m. as her 2nd husband, William, 1st Earl Amherst, and d. 20 July 1864.
(B.P. 1949 ed.)
(The hatchment of Earl Amherst's 1st wife is at Riverhead)

KNOWLTON

1. Sinister background black

On a shield with bow of ribbon above
Qly, 1st, Sable a griffin passant or between three crescents argent
(D'Aeth), 2nd, Sable a chevron between three fleurs-de-lys
argent (   ), 3rd, Sable on a chevron between three escallops argent
three horses' heads erased gules (   ), 4th, Gules a chief ermine
(Narborough), impaling, Azure three cross crosslets fitchy in bend
between two bendlets or (Knatchbull) Palm branches in base tied
with a gold tasselled cord
For Harriet, 3rd dau. of Sir Edward Knatchbull, 8th Bt., who m.
Admiral George William Hughes D'Aeth, of Knowlton Court, and d. 5
Aug. 1864.   (B.L.G. 1937 ed.)

LAMBERHURST

1. All black background

On a lozenge surmounted by a cherub's head
Sable a cross formy or voided azure (Matson)
Motto: Resurgam   On a mantle gules and argent   Skull below
For Margaret, dau. and co-heiress of William Matson. She d. 17 May
1827, aged 80.   (M.I.)

2. Sinister background black

Qly, 1st and 4th, Azure a griffin segreant or langued gules (Morland),
2nd and 3rd, Sable a cross formy or voided azure (Matson)   In
pretence: Qly, 1st and 4th, Sable two bars and in chief three escallops
or (Marriott), 2nd, Per fess embattled azure and gules three bezants
(Pearson), 3rd, Or a lion rampant gules langued azure (Bosworth)
Motto: Resurgam   Two cherubs' heads above
For Lydia Catherine, eldest dau. and co-heir of the Rev. James
Marriott, Rector of Horsmonden, who m. William Alexander Morland,
of Court Lodge, and d. 25 May 1843.   (B.L.G. 1937 ed.)

3. All black background

Qly, 1st and 4th, Sable a cross formy voided or (Matson), 2nd and 3rd,
Azure a griffin segreant or langued and clawed gules (Morland)
In pretence: As 2.
Crest: A falcon proper belled or jessed gules   Mantling: Gules and
argent   Motto: Resurgam
For William Alexander Morland, who d. 24 Dec. 1846.
(B.L.G. 1937 ed.)

LEEDS Castle

1. Dexter background black

Qly, 1st and 4th, Gules a lion rampant within an orle of cross crosslets and molets alternately or (Martin), 2nd and 3rd, Argent two chevronels sable between three roses gules (Wykeham)
Crests: Dexter, A martin entwined by a serpent proper, in the beak a cross crosslet fitchy or   Sinister, A buffalo's head erased sable charged on the neck with two chevronels argent   Mantling: Gules and argent
For Fiennes Wykeham-Martin, of Leeds Castle, who m. Eliza, dau. of Richard Bignell, and d. 14 Sept. 1840.   (B.L.G. 1937 ed.)

2. Sinister background black

Qly, 1st and 4th, Martin, with crescent argent for difference, 2nd and 3rd, Or two chevronels sable between three roses barbed and seeded gules (Wykeham), impaling, Qly, 1st and 4th, Sable on a fess embattled counterembattled or between three goats statant argent three roundels sable (Mann), 2nd and 3rd, Sable gutty argent on a fess or three choughs sable (Cornwallis)
Mantling: Gules and or   Motto: In coelo quies   Three cherubs' heads above
For Jemima Isabella, dau. of James, 5th Earl Cornwallis, who m. as his 1st wife, Charles Wykeham-Martin, of Leeds Castle, and d. 17 Dec. 1836.   (B.L.G. 1937 ed.)

3. Dexter and top sinister background black

Qly, 1st and 4th, Martin, as 1, 2nd and 3rd, Argent two chevronels sable between three roses gules barbed and seeded proper (Wykeham), impaling two coats per fess; in chief, Qly, 1st and 4th, Mann, 2nd and 3rd, Cornwallis, with fess argent, and in base, Vert three hinds courant argent attired or within a bordure argent (Trollope)
Crests: As 1.   Motto: Manners makyth man
For Charles Wykeham-Martin, of Leeds Castle, who m. 1st, Jemima Isabella (d. 17 Dec. 1836), dau. of James, 5th Earl Cornwallis, and 2nd, 1838, Matilda (d. 5 June 1876), dau. of Sir John Trollope, 6th Bt., and d. 30 Oct. 1870.   (B.L.G. 1937 ed.)

4. Sinister background black

Qly, 1st and 4th, Martin, as 1, 2nd and 3rd, Wykeham, as 1, impaling, Vert a fess engrailed ermine between in chief three boars' heads and in base a pheon vert (Ward)
Mantling: Gules and or   Motto: In coelo quies   Three cherubs' heads above
For Elizabeth, dau. of John Ward, who m. 1850, Philip Wykeham-Martin, of Leeds Castle, and d.
(B.L.G. 1937 ed.)

5. All black background
Qly, 1st and 4th, Martin, as 1, 2nd and 3rd, Wykeham, as 2, impaling,
Vert a fess engrailed or ermined sable between in chief three boars'
heads erased and in base a pheon or (Ward)
Crests: Dexter, As 1.   Sinister, A bull's head erased sable armed or
charged on the neck with two chevronels argent   Mantling: Gules
and or   Motto: In coelo quies
For Philip Wykeham-Martin, of Leeds Castle, who d. 31 May 1878.
(B.L.G. 1937 ed.)

LINTON

1. Sinister background black
Qly, 1st and 4th, Gules three tilting spears palewise in fess or headed
argent (Amherst), 2nd, Argent a bend gules a canton sable (Kerrill),
3rd, Azure three arrows points downwards or (Archer)   In pretence:
Qly, 1st and 4th, Sable gutty argent, on a fess argent three choughs
proper (Cornwallis), 2nd and 3rd, Sable on a fess embattled
counterembattled between three goats trippant argent three roundels
sable (Mann)
Viscountess's coronet   Supporters: Two Canadian War Indians, etc.
(see Riverhead 1.)
For Julia, only dau. of John, 5th Earl Cornwallis, who m. as his 1st
wife, 1862, William Archer, 3rd Earl Amherst, and d. 1 Sept. 1883.
(B.P. 1949 ed.)

LOOSE

1. Dexter background black
Gules crusilly a lion rampant or (Martin), impaling, Or three bars
gemel gules over all a lion rampant sable langued gules (Fairfax)
Crest: A martin argent beak, legs and feet gules, entwined by a serpent
proper   Mantling: Gules and argent   Motto: Mens conscia recti
For Denny Martin, who m. Frances, dau. of Thomas, 5th Baron
Fairfax, and d.   She d. 13 Dec. 1791.
(B.L.G. 1937 ed.; B.P. 1949 ed.)

2. All green background
Qly, 1st and 4th, Gules a lion rampant or (Martin), 2nd and 3rd,
Fairfax
Crest: On a chapeau gules and ermine a lion passant guardant sable
langued gules   Mantling and motto: As 1.
For the Rev. Denny Martin, D.D., who assumed the name of Fairfax on
succeeding to the estates of Leeds Castle, and d. 1800.   (Sources, as 1)

3. Sinister background black
Two cartouches   Dexter, Per pale or and sable a pheon
counterchanged (Whatman)   Sinister, Argent on a bend azure three
stags' heads cabossed or (Stanley)
Mantling: Gules and argent   Motto: Mors janua vitæ
Exterior of cartouches flanked by green branches and escallop above
A circular hatchment in narrow black frame
For Sarah, eldest dau. of Edward Stanley, who m. 1769, as his 1st
wife, James Whatman, of Vintners, Maidstone, and d. 1775.
(B.L.G. 2nd ed.)

LULLINGSTONE

1. All black background
Or three cinquefoils sable, the Badge of Ulster (Dyke)
Crest: A mailed cubit arm proper cuffed or holding a cinquefoil or
leaved and slipped vert   Mantling: Gules and argent   Motto:
Resurgam
For Sir Thomas Dyke, 4th Bt., who d. unm. 22 Nov. 1831.
(B.P. 1949 ed.)

2. Dexter background black
Dyke, with Badge of Ulster, impaling, Qly, 1st and 4th, Azure two
swords in chevron argent pommelled and hilted or between three
covered cups or (Jenner), 2nd and 3rd, Or a fess azure between
three crescents gules (Poe)
Crest: A mailed cubit arm proper cuffed or the hand proper holding a
cinquefoil slipped sable   Mantling: Gules and argent
Motto: Resurgam
For Sir Percival Hart Dyke, 5th Bt., who m. 1798, Anne, eldest dau. of
Robert Jenner, of Wenvoe Castle Glamorgan, and d. 4 Aug. 1846.
(Source, as 1.)

3. Dexter background black
Qly, 1st and 4th, Dyke, with Badge of Ulster in 1st quarter, 2nd, Per
chevron azure and gules three harts trippant or (Hart), 3rd, Azure a
lion rampant ermine tail forked langued and armed gules ducally
crowned or (Peche), impaling, Gules a bend barry of eight or and azure
between six crescents argent (Wells)
Crest: A mailed cubit arm holding a cinquefoil slipped sable
Mantling: Sable and or   Motto: In coelo quies
For Sir Percyvall Hart Dyke, 6th Bt., who m. 1835, Elizabeth, youngest
dau. of John Wells, of Bickley, Kent, and d. 12 Nov. 1875.
(Source, as 1.)

LYDD

1. Dexter background black
Azure three leopards' heads affronté couped at the shoulders or
(Denne), impaling, Argent a chevron between three cocks gules (Cobb)
Crest: A leopard's head as in the arms   Mantling: Gules and argent
Motto: Resurgam
For David Denne, who m. 1788, Katherine, dau. of Robert Cobb, and d.
Feb. 1819, aged 67. She d. 2 Sept. 1859.   (B.L.G. 5th ed.)

2. Sinister background black
Qly, 1st and 4th, Azure three bars ermine in chief three fleurs-de-lys or
(Denne), 2nd, Azure three leopards' heads affronté couped at the
shoulders or (Denne), 3rd, Argent two flaunches sable on each a
leopard's face or (Denne), impaling, Qly, 1st and 4th, Argent a chevron
between three cocks gules (Cobb), 2nd and 3rd, Argent a chevron
between three bulls' heads cabossed gules (Curteis)
Motto: In coelo quies
For Louisa Anne, dau. of the Rev. Thomas Cobb, who married David
Denne, and d. 1846.   He. d. 1861.   (B.L.G. 5th ed.; O.H.S.)

3. All black background
On a lozenge surmounted by a cherub's head
Argent a huntinghorn proper on a chief azure three molets argent
(Murray)   In pretence: Or a chevron gules between three lions
rampant sable langued gules on a chief sable three stags' heads argent
(Skinner)
Mantling: Gules and argent   Motto: In coelo quies
For Mary (née Skinner), who m. General Thomas Murray, and d.
8 July 1829.   (O.H.S.)

LYMINGE

1. Sinister background black
Argent a chevron between three hawks' heads erased azure
(Honywood), impaling, Or a cross formy fitchy gules on a chief sable
three fleurs-de-lys or (Brockman)
Motto: In coelo quies   Two cherubs' heads above
For Mary, sister of James Drake Brockman, of Beachborough, who m.
William Honywood, and d.   (B.P. 1949 ed.; Toke M.S.)

2. Dexter background black
Argent a chevron between three hawks' heads erased azure langued
gules (Honywood), impaling, Or a bend engrailed vert cotised
sable (Hanbury)

Crest: A wolf's head erased ermine langued gules   Mantling: Gules
and argent   Motto: Resurgam
For William Philip Honywood, of Marks Hall, Essex, who m. Priscilla
Hanbury, and d. 22 Apr. 1801.   (B.P. 1949 ed.)

LYNSTED

1. Sinister background black
Per fess azure and or a pale counterchanged three bucks' heads erased
or (Roper), impaling, Azure a chevron engrailed between three lions
passant guardant or (Smythe)
Baroness's coronet   Motto: Spes mea in Deo   Supporters:
Dexter, A buck or   Sinister, A heraldic tyger reguardant argent
For Catherine, dau. of Philip, 2nd Viscount Strangford, who m. as his
1st wife, Jan. 1703/4, Henry, 8th Baron Teynham, and d. 26 Apr.
1711.   (B.P. 1949 ed.)

2. Sinister background black
Roper, impaling, Per saltire vert and argent a saltire gules (Gage)
Baroness's coronet   Motto and supporters: As 1.
For Mary, dau. of Sir John Gage, 4th Bt., who m. as his 2nd wife,
Jan. 1715/16, Henry, 8th Baron Teynham, and d.s.p. Jan. 1716/17.
(B.P. 1949 ed.)

3. Dexter background black
Roper, impaling, Gules on a chevron or between three roundels argent
three roundels sable (Webber)
Baron's coronet   Crest: A lion rampant sable holding a ducal
coronet or   Mantling (slight); Gules and argent   Motto: As 1.
Supporters: Dexter, as 1. Sinister, A Bengal tiger reguardant proper
For Henry, 11th Baron Teynham, who m. 2nd, 1760, Elizabeth, widow
of John Mills, and dau. of Joseph Webber, and d. 10 Dec. 1786.
(B.P. 1949 ed.)

4. All black background
On a lozenge, surmounted by a baroness's coronet   Arms: As 3.
Motto: As 1.   Supporters: Dexter, as 1.   Sinister, A wolf
reguardant proper
For Elizabeth, widow of Henry, 11th Baron Teynham, d. 4 Nov. 1793.
(B.P. 1949 ed.)

5. All black background
Roper arms only
Baron's coronet   Crest: As 3.   Motto: As 1.   Supporters:
Dexter, as 1.   Sinister, A heraldic tyger reguardant proper   All
on a mantle gules and ermine

Probably for Philip, 9th Baron, d. unm. 13 June 1727; Henry, 12th
Baron, d. unm. 10 Jan. 1800; or John, 13th Baron, d. unm. 6 Sept.
1824.   (B.P. 1963 ed.)

6. All black background
Roper arms only
Baron's coronet   Crest: As 3.   Motto: As 1.   Supporters:
Dexter, as 1.   Sinister, A Bengal tiger reguardant argent
Mantling: Gules and ermine
For attribution, see 5.

7. All black background
Roper arms only
Baron's coronet   Crest: As 3.   Motto: As 1.   Supporters:
Dexter as 1.   Sinister, A heraldic tyger reguardant argent   All
on a mantle gules and ermine
For attribution, see 5.

8. Sinister background black
Argent three lozenge buckles tongues fesswise gules, a molet sable for
difference (Jerningham), impaling, Roper   Cherub's head above
and on each side of shield
For Elizabeth, dau. of Christopher, 5th Baron Teynham, who m.
Charles Jerningham, and d.   (B.P. 1875 ed.)

9. Sinister background black
Sable on a fess or between three cats passant argent striped sable a
cross formy between two crescents gules (Tyler), impaling, Roper
Motto: Resurgam   Two cherubs' heads above shield
For Betty Maria, dau. of Henry, 11th Baron Teynham, who m. 1785,
Francis Henry Tyler, of Linsted Lodge, and d. 1 Mar. 1788, aged 26.
(B.P. 1949 ed.; M.I.)

10. All black background
Argent on a mount vert an oak tree proper between two boars erect
sable armed or (Hugessen)   In pretence, and impaling, Azure a fess
dancetty between three cherubs' heads or (Adye)
Crest: An oak tree proper between two wings per pale azure and or
Mantling: Gules and argent   Motto: Mortendo vivo
For William Hugessen, of Provender, who m. Elizabeth, dau. of James
Adye, and d. 1719.   She d. 1725.   (B.L.G. 2nd ed.)
(In view of the background possibly also used subsequently for
his widow)

11. Sinister background black
Argent on a mount vert an oak tree proper fructed or between two
boars erect sable armed or (Hugessen), impaling, Per saltire argent and
sable a bordure counterchanged (Gott)

Crest: An oak tree proper fructed or between two wings azure edged or
Mantling: Gules and argent   Motto: In coelo quies
For Martha, dau. of Peter Gott, of Stanmer, Sussex, who m. as his 1st
wife, William Hugessen, and d. 15 Mar. 1733, aged 55.
(B.L.G. 2nd ed.; M.I.)

12. Sinister background black
Qly, 1st and 4th, Argent on a mount vert an oak tree proper fructed or
between two boars erect sable tusked or (Hugessen), 2nd and 3rd,
Azure a fess dancetty between three cherubs' heads argent winged or
(Adye), impaling, Or on a chevron azure between three French
marigolds slipped proper two lions passant respectant or (Tyssen)
Crest: A tree proper between two wings azure edged or   Mantling:
Gules and argent
For Dorothy, dau. of Francis Tyssen, of Hackney, who m. as his 2nd
wife, William Hugessen, and d. 23 May 1749, aged 55.   (Sources, as 11).

13. All black background
Per saltire argent and sable a bordure counterchanged (Gott), impaling,
Tyssen   In pretence (over impalement line): Qly, 1st and 4th,
Hugessen, as 11, 2nd and 3rd, Adye, as 10.
Peer's helm   Crest: An oak tree proper between two wings azure
edged or   Mantling: Gules and argent
Probably for William Hugessen, who m. 1st, Martha, dau. of Peter Gott,
and 2nd, Dorothy, dau. of Francis Tyssen, and d. 18 Jan. 1753,
aged 52.   (Sources, as 11.)
(If for William Hugessen, a most remarkable form of marshalling!)

14. Dexter background black
Qly, 1st and 4th, Hugessen, as 12, 2nd and 3rd, Adye, as 10, impaling,
Argent a chevron between three hawks' heads erased azure (Honywood)
Crest: On a mount vert an oak tree proper between two wings azure
edged or   Mantling: Gules and argent
For William Western Hugessen, of Provender, who m. Thomasine,
dau of Sir John Honywood, 3rd Bt., and d. 1764.
(B.L.G. 2nd ed.; B.P. 1939 ed.)

15. All black background
Hugessen arms only, as 10, with crescent sable for difference
Crest: A tree proper between two wings or   Mantling: Gules and
argent   Motto: Resurgam   Skull and crossbones in base,
and cherubs' heads at top corners of shield
Unidentified

16. Sinister background black
Azure three cross crosslets fitchy in bend between two bendlets or
(Knatchbull), impaling, Argent a chevron between three hawks' heads
erased azure beaked or (Honywood)

Motto: Resurgam   Shield suspended from a lover's knot and
flanked by cherub's heads, with laurel branches at base
For Annabella Christiana, dau. of Sir John Honywood, 4th Bt., who m.
1806, as his 1st wife, Sir Edward Knatchbull, 9th Bt., and d. 4 Apr.
1814.   (B.P. 1949 ed.)

17. All black background
Sable a fess or between three cinquefoils argent, in chief a label of three
points or for difference (Eve), impaling, Sable a fess dancetty between
three cherubs' heads or (Adye)
Crest: A horse passant argent   Mantling: Gules and argent
Motto: Virtus in actione consistit   On a wood panel
Frame inscribed: Henry Eve, M.D. ob July 1686, Interred the 31st,
Aet. 31. Dorothy Eve, wife of Henry Eve, M.D. ob. Nov. 1691.
Interred Dec. 1.

18. Sinister background black
Sable a fess or between three cinquefoils argent, in chief a crescent or
for difference (Eve)   In pretence, and impaling, Eve, without
crescent
Crest and mantling: As 17.   Motto: . itae medio . . primur
Frame inscribed: Mrs. Dorothy Eve, the wife of Charles Eve of
Canterbury, Gent, died June ye 16th 1755. Interred here the 26th
instant aged 31 years.
(M.I. confirms above details; she was dau. and heiress of Henry Eve)

MAIDSTONE, All Saints

1. All black background
Or two chevrons gules, on a canton gules a molet or (Pope), impaling,
Ermine a lion rampant azure (Hollands)
Crest: A tiger statant proper, langued gules, collared and chain
reflexed over back or   Mantling: Gules and argent   Motto: In
coelo quies
For Thomas Pope, who m. Ann Hollands and d. 19 July 1748, aged 77.
She d. Oct. 1747, aged 64.   (Berry)

Museum

1. Dexter background black
Argent in chief two cross crosslets fitchy and in base a cinquefoil sable,
a crescent gules for difference (Best), impaling, Sable a fess engrailed
between three whelkshells or (Shelley)

Crest: From a mural coronet a demi-ostrich rising argent, in the beak a cross crosslet fitchy sable   Mantling: Gules and argent
Motto: Mors janua vitæ
For James Best, of Park House, Boxley, who m. Frances, dau. and co-heir of Richard Shelley, of Michelgrove, Sussex, and d. 29 Jan. 1782. (B.L.G. 1937 ed.)

2. Dexter background black
Sable in chief two cross crosslets fitchy and in base a cinquefoil argent, a crescent on a crescent for difference (Best), impaling to dexter, Or fretty vert (   ), and to sinister, Argent
Crest: From a mural coronet a demi-ostrich rising argent, in the beak a cross crosslet fitchy or   Mantling: Gules and argent
Motto: Resurgam
For James Best, 2nd son of 1, who m. 1st, Elizabeth — , and 2nd, Hannah Middleton, and d.s.p. 10 Dec. 1828.   (B.L.G. 1937 ed.)

3. Dexter background black
Sable in chief two cross crosslets fitchy and in base a cinquefoil or (Best), impaling, Azure on a chevron argent between three fleurs-de-lys or three molets gules (Sheppard)
Crest and mantling: As 2.   Motto: In coelo quies   Skull in base
Unidentified
(This hatchment is now missing)

4. All black background
On a lozenge   Per saltire gules and argent a saltire between four cross crosslets all counterchanged, in centre chief the Badge of Ulster (Twisden)   In pretence: Argent on a mount vert three trees proper, on a chief azure three doves argent (Wildash)
Motto: In coelo quies
For Rebecca, dau. and co-heiress of Isaac Wildash, who m. Sir Roger Twisden, 6th Bt., and d. 3 Feb. 1833. He d. 1779.
(B.E.B.; N. E. Toke; G.E.C.)

5. Dexter background black
Twisden, but per saltire argent and gules, with Badge or Ulster in dexter chief, impaling, Qly, 1st and 4th, Gules two bars or charged with three mascles two and one azure, on a canton argent an anchor with rope reflexed sable (Geary), 2nd and 3rd, Argent two chevronels between three fleurs-de-lys and a bordure gules (Barber)
Crest: A cockatrice wings displayed sable and or, langued gules, comb, wattles and feet or   Mantling: Gules and argent   Motto: In coelo quies
Skull below
For Sir John Papillon Twisden, 7th Bt., who m. Elizabeth, dau. of Admiral Sir Francis Geary, Bt., and d. 10 Feb. 1810.
(Sources, as 4.)

6. Sinister background black
Twisden, As 5, with Badge of Ulster in fess point and a crescent sable
in chief for difference, impaling, Vert a fess dancetty or between
three swans argent beaked and legged or (Coppard)
Motto: In coelo quies   Cherub's head at each top angle of shield,
which is suspended from a lover's knot
For Catherine Judith, dau. of the Rev. William Coppard, D.D., who
m. Sir John Twisden, 8th Bt., and d. 29 Apr. 1819.   (Sources, as 4.)

7. All black background
Qly, 1st and 4th, Azure three swans' heads erased argent langued gules
(Hedges), 2nd and 3rd, Per pale gules and azure a chevron ermine
between three lions rampant or (   )
Crest: A swan's head erased argent   Mantling: Gules and argent
Motto: Omne solum patria
For William Hedges, who d.s.p. 23 May 1734, aged 57.   (O.H.S.)
(This hatchment is now missing)

8. Sinister background black
Per fess azure and or a pale counterchanged and three lions rampant
guardant or (Wheatley), impaling, Per pale gules and sable three stags'
heads erased or (Lewin)
Motto: In morte victor
For Margaret Salisbury, dau. and co-heir of Edmond Lewin, who m.
1697, as his 2nd wife, John Wheatley, of Erith, and d. 27 May 1743.
(B.L.G. 1937 ed.)
(This hatchment is now missing)

9. All black background
Gules an eagle displayed ermine a chief chequy or and sable (Hasted),
impaling, Argent on a chevron sable three garbs or, on a canton gules a
fret or (Yardley)
Crest: An eagle displayed ermine   Mantling: Gules and argent
A very small hatchment, c. 1 ft. x 1 ft.
For Joseph Hasted, who m. Catherine Yardley, and d. 1732.   (O.H.S.)

10. All black background
Hasted arms only
Crest and mantling: As 9.
Unidentified

11. All black background
On a lozenge   Argent a chevron between three pierced molets
sable (   )   In pretence: Argent a griffin passant sable armed and
langued gules (   )
Unidentified
(Hatchments 1–3 were formerly in Boxley church, 4–6 in East Malling
church, 7 and 8 in Erith church, and 11 in East Fairleigh church)

MARGATE

1. All black background
Per chevron gules and sable in chief two spoonbills respectant proper
and in base a fish naiant or (Cobb), impaling, Argent three bendlets
azure (   )
Crest: A spoonbill's head erased proper holding in the bill a fish or
Mantling: Gules and argent   Motto: Mors janua vitæ
Unidentified

2. All black background
Cobb, as 1, impaling three coats, two in chief per pale and one in base,
1. Azure two lions' gambs addorsed erect proper between nine
fleurs-de-lys or (Chippendale), 2. Paly of six or and azure on a canton
azure a fleur-de-lys or (   ), 3. Argent a fret gules a chief azure
(Curwen)
Crest: A spoonbill's head erased with fish in bill proper   Mantling:
Gules and argent   Motto; Mors janua vitæ
For Francis Cobb, who m. 1st, Elizabeth Chippendale, d. 1787, 2nd,
Mary, dau. of Thomas Blackburn, d. 1802, 3rd, Charlotte Mary
Blackburn-Curwen, d. 1823, and d. 13 Aug. 1831.   (G.M.)

3. Dexter background black
Per fess gules and or in base an olive tree eradicated proper, in chief the
head and forelegs of a crocodile issuant proper (Dalbiac), impaling
to dexter, Argent, and to sinister, Gules two bars or (Harcourt)
Crest: A dove with olive branch in beak proper   Mantling: Gules
and argent   Motto (above crest, and only partly legible): Pa —
Supporters: Two wild men each with a club on his shoulder proper
Unidentified

4. Dexter background black
Two oval shields   Dexter, within the Order of the Bath, Argent on a
fess azure cotised engrailed sable three crescents argent, in centre chief
two lions rampant respectant gules supporting an anchor sable, on a canton
gules the Badge of the Sicilian Order of St Ferdinand of Merit (Staines)
Sinister, Staines, impaling, Qly, 1st and 4th, Or on a pale gules a sword
erect argent hilted or, on a chief azure three bezants (Bargrave), 2nd
and 3rd, Argent a chevron between three oxen sable (Tournay)
Crest: From a naval coronet or a stag's head couped qly argent and or
attired and langued gules   Mantling: Azure and argent   Motto:
Virtute ad astra   Three badges of Orders pendent below
dexter shield   Skull and crossbones in base
For Sir Thomas Staines, R.N., K.C.B., Knight Commander of the
Royal Sicilian Order of St Ferdinand and Knight of the Imperial
Ottoman Order of the Crescent. He m. 1819, Sarah, youngest dau. of
Robert Tournay Bargrave, of Eastry Court, and d. 13 July 1830.
(D.N.B.; M.I.)

5. Background black behind dexter shield, lozenge and sinister side of sinister shield
A lozenge flanked by two shields   Dexter, an oval shield within
Order of the Bath, Staines   Lozenge, Staines, with in pretence, Qly,
1st and 4th, Bargrave, 2nd and 3rd, Tournay   Sinister shield, Gules
on a fess between three doves argent three crosses formy gules, in
chief a medal argent stringed sable (Gunning) In pretence: Qly, 1st and
4th, Bargrave, 2nd and 3rd, Tournay
Three medals or badges of orders pendent between dexter shield and
lozenge   Lozenge surmounted by two cherubs' heads
For Sarah, widow of Sir Thomas Staines, and wife of George Gunning.
She d. 25 Jan. 1832.   (Sources, as 4.)
(There is another hatchment for Sarah Gunning in Eastry church)

6. Dexter background black
Or on a bend gules three cross crosslets fitchy argent, in the sinister
chief a pelican in her piety with three young proper (Taddy), impaling,
Azure a chevron or between three lions rampant argent (   )
Crest: A fleur-de-lys argent   Mantling: Gules and argent
Motto: Labor ipse voluptas
Unidentified

7. Dexter background black
Lozengy azure and or on a chief gules three lions rampant or langued
sable (Baker), impaling, Per chevron or and argent a lion rampant sable
within a bordure gules charged with eight roundels argent (Burnell)
Crest: A demi-unicorn argent, maned, armed and unguled or
Mantling: Gules and argent   Motto: Resurgam
Unidentified

8. Dexter background black
Or a griffin segreant sable within a bordure gules (Boys), impaling, Per
chevron azure and argent in chief two birds volant or (Stephens)
Crest: A demi-lion rampant crowned or issuing from a chapeau gules
and ermine   Mantling: Gules and argent   Motto: Spectemur agendo
For John Boys, who m. 1804, Martha (d. 12 Aug. 1861), dau. of the
Rev. Athelstan Stephens, and d. 13 Jan. 1861.
(M.I.; B.L.G. 2nd ed.)

9. All black background
Boys, impaling, Qly argent and azure on a cross or five annulets sable,
in the first and fourth quarters an ermine spot (Osborne)
Crest, mantling and motto: As 8.
For John Harvey Boys, who m. 1839, Mary, dau. of Latham Osborn,
and d. 1883. She d. 1868.   (B.L.G. 2nd ed.; J. Tindale)

10. Sinister background black
Or a fess wavy between six billets sable (Dowdeswell)   In pretence:

Qly, 1st and 4th, Per saltire sable and argent a lion rampant
counterchanged (Payne), 2nd, Argent on a bend sable three dolphins
embowed argent crowned or (Rolte), 3rd, Azure a chevron ermine
between three swans argent (   )
Motto: In coelo quies   Two cherubs' heads above shield and
skull below
Possibly for Anne Payne, who m. 1727, George Dowdeswell, and d.
(Canterbury Marriage Licences)

11. Dexter background black
Sable on a cross formy throughout per bend sinister ermine and or a
quatrefoil counterchanged (Slack), impaling, Sable a bull statant
guardant argent (   )
Crest: A snail proper   Mantling: Gules and argent   Motto: In
coelo quies   Winged skull below
Unidentified

12. Sinister background black
Vert fretty argent (   )   In pretence: Sable a chevron or
ermined sable between three millrinds or, on a chief argent a lion
passant gules (Turner)
Motto: Resurgam   Shield surmounted by a cherub's head
For Ann, dau. and heiress of Capt. David Turner, relict of James
Brown, who m. Jacob Sawkins, and d. 1 Feb. 1810.   (M.I.)

13. All black background
On a lozenge surmounted by a cherub's head
Qly, 1st and 4th, Gules a griffin passant and a chief or (Brown),
2nd and 3rd, Turner, millrinds argent
Probably for Ann Turner Brown, only child of James Brown, of Chapel
Hill House, and grand-daughter of Capt. David Turner, of Nash
Court, d. 5 Mar. 1838, aged 68.   (M.I.)

14. Sinister background black
Gules on a chevron argent a lion rampant sable (Brooke), impaling,
Argent a bend azure fretty or (   )
Motto: In coelo quies   Shield surmounted by two cherubs' heads,
and skull in base
Unidentified

15. All black background
Brooke arms only, on a lozenge surmounted by a cherub's head
Motto: Mors janua vitæ   Skull in base
For Ann, dau. of Robert Brooke, d. 12 Mar. 1787, aged 63.   (M.I.)

16. Sinister background black
Azure a saltire or a crescent argent for difference (Slater), impaling,

Argent on a cross azure five pheons argent, on a chief azure two
demi-lions rampant argent (   )
No motto   Shield suspended from gilt ribbons
For Frances, wife of George Slater, d. 24 Apr. 1817, aged 75. He d.
1 Dec. 1822, aged 84.   (M.I.)

17. Dexter background black
Argent a chevron azure between three buglehorns stringed sable
(Forster), impaling to dexter, Forster, impaling to sinister, Gules ten
billets or, a bordure argent charged with roundels azure and gules
alternately (Salter)
Crests (both on same wreath): Dexter, A stag statant sable ermined
argent attired or   Sinister, An arm embowed in armour argent
holding in the hand a spear broken at the top, shafted gules, headed
argent   Mantling: Gules and argent   Motto: Quo feret
fortuna paratus
For Francis Forster, who d. 24 Feb. 1835, aged 63. His widow,
Margaret, d. 30 Apr. 1854, aged 83.   (M.I.)

18. Dexter background black
Or a tree in leaf on a mount vert, on a chief argent three crosses argent
(   ), impaling, Per bend sinister rompu argent and sable six
martlets counterchanged (Allen)
No crest   Mantling: Gules and argent   Motto: Resurgam
Unidentified

19. Dexter background black
Azure a hawk close proper standing on a mount vert, on a chief gules a
crescent between two molets or (   ), impaling, Argent three
boars' heads couped sable langued gules armed or (   )
Crest: A demi-wyvern wings raised and holding a sword argent hilted
or, issuing from a celestial crown or balls argent   Mantling: Gules
and argent
Unidentified

20. All black background
Barry of ten argent and azure six escutcheons three, two and one sable,
each charged with a lion rampant or (Cecil)
To dexter of main shield, Cecil, with in pretence, Sable two chevronels
and a chief ermine (   ) S.Bl.   To sinister of main shield,
Cecil, impaling, Or a pile engrailed sable (   ) A.Bl.
Crest: On a chapeau gules and ermine two lions rampant respectant, the
dexter argent the sinister azure, supporting a garb or   Mantling:
Gules and argent   Motto: Resurgam   Winged skull in base
Unidentified

MEOPHAM

1. All black background
Qly, 1st and 4th, Qly gules and or ermined sable in the first and fourth
a lion rampant argent, over all a fess azure charged with three martlets
or, the Badge of Ulster (Bayley), 2nd and 3rd, Qly gules and or a
label of three points sable each point charged with three bezants
(Kennett), impaling, Per pale indented ermine and sable, on a chevron
gules three crosses formy fitchy argent (Markett)
Crest: On a mount vert behind a wall a lion rampant argent armed and
langued gules   Mantling: Gules and argent   Motto: Deus nobis
For the Rt. Hon. Sir John Bayley, 1st Bt., who m. Elizabeth, youngest
dau. of John Markett, of Meopham Court Lodge, and d. 23 Jan. 1837,
aged 77.   (M.I.; B.P. 1875 ed.)

MERSHAM

1. Dexter background black
Azure three cross crosslets fitchy between two bendlets or, in sinister
chief the Badge of Ulster (Knatchbull), impaling, Qly, 1st and 4th,
Ermine a lion rampant gules collared argent, on a chief azure three roses
argent (Russell), 2nd and 3rd, Azure a bend engrailed or ermined sable
between two crescents or, a canton gules (Watts)
Crest: On a chapeau gules and ermine an ounce statant argent spotted
sable   Mantling: Gules and argent   Motto: In crucifixia gloria mea
For Sir Norton Joseph Knatchbull, 10th Bt., who m. 1831, Mary, dau.
of Jesse Watts-Russell, of Ilam Hall, Staffs, and d. 2 Feb. 1868.
(B.P. 1875 ed.)

MILTON, nr. Gravesend

1. All black background
Azure crusilly or a lion rampant guardant argent, a chief barry nebuly
of four or and sable (Dalton)
Crest: A dragon's head with wings displayed vert, the wings lined or,
collared nebuly argent   Mantling: Gules and argent
For Thomas Dalton, of Parrock House, Milton, Col. of the West Kent
Regiment of Militia, d. at Rome, 24 Feb. 1827, aged 67.   (M.I.)

MINSTER-IN-SHEPPEY

1. All black background
Sable on a cross between four fleurs-de-lys or five arches sable, in

centre point a fleur-de-lys and in chief a label for cadency (Banks)
Crest: A stork argent beaked gules standing on a fallen pillar argent,
resting its dexter claw on a fleur-de-lys or   Mantling: Gules
and argent   Motto: Resurgam
To dexter of main shield, Banks impaling a blank S.Bl.   To sinister
of main shield, Banks impaling, Qly gules and ermine in the first and
fourth quarters a goat's head erased argent armed or (Morton) D.Bl.
For John Banks, of Sheppey Court, who m. 1st, Elizabeth, dau. of
F. Ladd, and 2nd, Fanny, dau. of G. Morton, and d. 5 Nov. 1835.
(B.L.G. 1906 ed.; M.I.)

2. Sinister background black
Sable on a cross between four fleurs-de-lys or five arches sable, in
centre point a fleur-de-lys sable (Banks)
Motto: Resurgam   Two cherub's heads above
Probably for Eliza Jane, wife of Delamark Banks, of Sheppey Court.
She d. 12 Apr. 1841.   (Sources, as 1.)

MONKTON

1. All black background
Argent two flaunches sable each charged with a leopard's face or
(Denne) To dexter of main shield, Denne, impaling, Per fess or and
argent three Moors' heads couped proper wreathed at the temples
argent and sable (Collard) S.Bl.   To sinister of main shield,
Denne, impaling, Azure a saltire or (Slater) D.Bl.
Crest: A stag lodged proper attired or   Mantling: Gules and argent
Cherub's head at each top corner of shield   Motto: Resurgemus
Winged skull in base
For Thomas Denne, of Ville of Sarre, who m. 1st, Mary, only child of
Henry Collard, of Monkton, and 2nd, Mary, dau. of George Slater,
of Margate, and d. 16 Mar. 1821.   (M.I.)

NONINGTON

1. All black background
Argent on a chevron between three roundels sable each charged with a
martlet argent three escallops or, all within a bordure engrailed vert
(Hammond), impaling, Gules two bends ermine (Kingsford)
Crest: An eagle's head erased argent langued gules enfiled with a collar
spiked or   Mantling: Gules and argent   Motto: In coelo quies
Probably for Anthony Hammond, of St Alban's Court, who m. Catherine
Kingsford, and was bur. 18 Jan. 1722-3.   (B.L.G. 1937 ed.; P.R.)

2. All black background
Hammond   In pretence: Argent a lion rampant gules armed and
langued sable between three pheons sable (Egerton)
Crest: An eagle's head erased sable langued and collared gules
Mantling: Gules and argent   Motto: Mors janua vitæ
For William Hammond, of St Alban's Court, who m. Charlotte, dau.
and co-heiress of William Egerton, and was bur. 14 May 1773.
(Sources, as 1.)

3. Dexter background black
Qly, 1st and 4th, Hammond, 2nd and 3rd, Egerton   In pretence:
Qly, 1st, Argent a chevron between three cinquefoils gules (Beauvoir),
2nd, Argent on a bend sable three molets or (   ), 3rd, Sable on
a chevron argent three buckles or (   ), 4th, Or a griffin segreant
sable taloned and langued gules within a bordure gules semy of billets
and acorns or (Boys)
Crest: An eagle's head erased sable beaked or langued gules gorged with
a collar wavy or   Mantling: Gules and argent   Motto: Resurgam
Skull in base
For William Hammond, of St Alban's Court, who m. 1785, Elizabeth,
dau. and co-heiress of Osmond Beauvoir, D.D. of Canterbury, and
d. 20 Nov. 1821.   (B.L.G. 1937 ed.; M.I.)

4. Dexter background black
Per fess, 1st, Hammond, 2nd, Egerton, impaling, Argent a chevron
gules between three oxen passant sable (Oxenden)
Crest: An eagle's head erased sable beaked or langued gules enfiled with
a collar gules, spiked or   Mantling and motto: As 1.
For William Osmund Hammond, of St Alban's Court, who m. 1815,
Mary Graham, dau. of Sir Henry Oxenden, 7th Bt. of Broome Park,
Kent, and d. 8 Feb. 1863.   (B.L.G. 1937 ed.)

NORTHBOURNE

1. Dexter background black
Qly of 16, 1st, Or a fess dancetty between three cross crosslets fitchy
gules, a crescent argent in chief for difference (Sandys), 2nd, Per
fess gules and azure a tower argent (Rawson), 3rd, Per pale argent and
azure a lion rampant per pale gules and or langued sable (Champneys),
4th, Argent on a fess between six annulets gules a bezant (Avenall),
5th, Gules a griffin segreant or langued sable (Tortes), 6th, Argent
a chevron gules between three eagles displayed vert (Blundell), 7th,
Sandys, no crescent, 8th, Rawson, 9th, Or a fess dancetty azure charged
on each upper point with a bezant between three billets azure each
charged with a lion passant guardant or (Rolle), 10th, Argent a chevron

between three swans sable (Yeo), 11th, Azure three crossbows or
(Sacheville), 12th, Argent two chevronels sable (Ashe), 13th, Gules a
chevron ermine between three pineapples or (Pyne), 14th, Gules a chief
indented argent (Brightley), 15th, Vert a lion rampant guardant
ermine debruised by a fess gules (Jewe), 16th, Argent a chevron sable
in dexter chief a trefoil slipped sable (Foote)   In pretence: Argent
three cocks gules (Chick)
Crest: A griffin segreant per fess or and gules charged on the shoulder
with a crescent gules   Mantling: Gules and argent   Motto:
Resurgam   Skull in base
For Edwin Humphrey Sandys, of Kingston, son of Richard Sandys of
Northbourne, who m. 2nd, Helen, dau. and heir of Edward Lord
Chick, and d.   (B.L.G. 1937 ed. — Sandys-Lumsdaine)

2. All black background
On a lozenge surmounted by a cherub's head
Qly of 16, 1st, Sandys without crescent, 2nd, Rawson, 3rd, Champneys,
4th, Avenall, 5th, Tortes, 6th, Blundell, 7th, Sandys as 1st, 8th,
Rawson, 9th, Rolle, 10th, Yeo, swans beaked argent, 11th, Sacheville,
12th, Ashe, 13th, Pyne, 14th, Brightley, 15th, Jewe, 16th, Foote
In pretence: Chick
Mantling: Gules and argent   No motto   Skull below
For Helen, widow of Edwin Humphrey Sandys. She d.
(Source, as 1.)

NORTON

1. All black background
On a lozenge   Sable a chevron between three pelicans' heads erased
or (Godfrey), impaling, Argent three picks sable (Pigott)
The lozenge is surrounded with decorative scrollwork and hangs
from an uncut mantle, gules and argent, which covers the whole
background except the extreme edge
For Mary, dau. and heir of Baptist Pigott, who m. Benjamin Godfrey,
of Norton Court, and d. 7 May 1730. He d. 13 Mar. 1704.   (M.I.)

OTFORD

1. All black background (should be dexter black)
Argent on a bend gules three cross crosslets or a crescent azure for
difference (Polhill), impaling, Ermine three boars' heads erect and
erased or armed argent langued gules (Borrett)

Crest: From a mural coronet gules a hind's head argent between two branches vert   Mantling: Gules and argent   Motto: Mors janua vitæ

For David Polhill, who m. 3rd, Elizabeth, dau. of John Borrett, of Shoreham, Kent, and d. 15 Jan. 1754.   (B.L.G. 1952 ed.; M.I.)

2. All black background

On a lozenge surmounted by a cherub's head

Polhill, no crescent, impaling, Sable ermined argent three boars' heads erect and erased or armed or langued gules (Borrett)

Motto: In coelo quies   Skull in base

For Elizabeth, widow of David Polhill, d. 28 Feb. 1785.

(Sources, as 1.)

3. Sinister background black

Polhill, as 2, impaling, Sable a fess engrailed between three whelk shells or (Shelley)

Motto: Mors janua vitæ   Shield surrounded by decorative scrollwork and surmounted by a cherub's head

For Tryphena, 3rd dau. of Sir John Shelley, Bt., of Michelgrove, Sussex, who m. as his 1st wife, Charles Polhill, of Chipstead Place, and d. 3 July 1756.   (Sources, as 1.)

4. Sinister background black

Qly of six, 1st and 6th, Or on a bend gules three cross crosslets or (Polhill), 2nd, Argent an eagle displayed azure langued gules (Buckland), 3rd, Azure a fess between three garbs or (Sandbach), 4th, Gules six cross crosslets, three, two and one or (Theobald), 5th, Ermine two pallets gules (Ireton), impaling, Argent a chevron between three lions' heads erased sable (Haswell)

Motto: Resurgam   Cherubs' heads above shield

For Patience, dau. of Thomas Haswell, who m. 1766, as his 2nd wife, Charles Polhill, and d. 16 Apr. 1803.   (B.L.G. 1952 ed.; M.I. gives 23 Apr. and name of wife as Hasswell)

5. All black background

Qly of six, 1st and 6th, Polhill, as 4, 2nd, Argent an eagle displayed sable (Buckland), 3rd, Sandbach, 4th, Theobald, 5th, Ireton, impaling to the dexter, Shelley, and to the sinister, Haswell

Crest: From a mural coronet or a hind's head proper between two branches vert   Mantling: Gules and argent   Motto: Spes mihi Christus

For Charles Polhill, who d. 23 July 1805, aged 85.   (Sources, as 1.)

6. Dexter background black

Qly, 1st, Polhill, as 4, 2nd, Argent an eagle displayed sable beaked and armed or (Buckland), 3rd, Sandbach, 4th, Theobald, impaling, Azure

a book or between in chief two molets and in base a saltire couped
argent (Porteous)
Crest: From a mural coronet or a hind's head proper between two oak
branches vert fructed or   Mantling: Gules and argent
Motto: Resurgam
For George Polhill, of Chipstead Place, who m. 1804, Mary, dau. of
Robert Porteous, of Southampton, and d. 13 Sept. 1839, aged 72.
(Sources, as 1.)

7. All black background
On a lozenge surmounted by a cherub's head
Qly, 1st, Polhill, as 4, 2nd, Buckland, as 5, 3rd, Sandbach, 4th,
Theobald, impaling, Porteous
For Mary, widow of George Polhill, d. 21 Feb. 1847.   (Sources, as 1.)

8. All black background
On a lozenge surrounded by ornamental gilt scrollwork
Polhill arms only, as 4.
Motto: In coelo quies
Possibly for Elizabeth, dau. of David Polhill and 3rd wife, Elizabeth
Barrett.   (Sources, as 1.)

OTTERDEN

1. Dexter background black
Qly, 1st and 4th, Vert on a fess argent three lions rampant vert
(Wheler), 2nd and 3rd, Argent a maunch sable (Hastings), impaling,
Sable a chevron between three lions passant or (Tattersall)
Crest: From a mural coronet or a griffin's head argent beaked or
Mantling: Gules and argent   Motto: In solido rursus locavit Deus
For Granville Hastings Wheler, who m. Jane, dau. of the Rev. William
de Chair Tattersall, and d. 1827. She d. 1843.   (B.L.G. 2nd ed.; O.H.S.)

EAST PECKHAM

1. Dexter background black
Per saltire argent and gules a saltire per saltire between four cross
crosslets all counterchanged, the Badge of Ulster (Twysden), impaling,
Argent on a fess gules three cross crosslets argent, on a canton azure
five fleurs-de-lys or (Wynch)
Crest: A cockatrice sejant gules, combed, winged and legged or
Morro: Resurgam   Skull in base
For Sir William Jervis Twysden, 7th Bt., who m. 1786, Frances, dau. of
Alexander Wynch, and d. 3 Feb. 1834.   (B.P. 1963 ed.)

WEST PECKHAM

1. All black background
Ermine a fess gules between three wolves' heads erased azure langued
gules, in centre chief the Badge of Ulster (Miller), impaling, Ermine on a
bend sable two hands and arms issuing out of clouds at the elbow all
proper rending a horseshoe or (Borlase)
Crest: A wolf's head erased azure langued gules collared ermine
Mantling: Gules and argent   Motto: Post funera virtus
For Sir Humphrey Miller, 1st Bt., who m. Mary, dau. of Sir John
Borlase, of Stratton, Bucks, and d. Aug. 1709.   (B.E.B.)

2. All black background
Miller, no Badge of Ulster
Crest and mantling: As 1.   Motto: Morior ut . uam
Possibly for Nicholas, eldest son of Sir Humphrey Miller, 1st Bt., who
d. 11 Feb. 1704.   (P.R.)

3. Dexter background black
Or three goats' heads erased sable (Bartholomew)   In pretence, and
impaling, Qly, 1st and 4th, Miller, 2nd and 3rd, Borlase
Crest: A demi-goat rampant argent, around the neck a branch vert
Mantling: Gules and argent   Motto: In morte quies
For Leonard Bartholomew, of Rochester, who m. Elizabeth, dau. and
heiress of Sir Humphrey Miller, Bt., and d. Jan. 1720.
(B.E.B.; Hasted; P.R.)

4. All black background
On a lozenge   Arms: As 3.
For Elizabeth, widow of Leonard Bartholomew, d. 2 May 1720.
(Sources, as 3.)

5. Sinister background black
Qly, 1st and 4th, Bartholomew, 2nd and 3rd, qly i. & iv. Miller, ii. & iii.
Borlase   In pretence and impaling, Argent on a bend engrailed
gules three trefoils slipped argent (Knowe)
Motto: In morte quies   Skull above shield
For Mary, dau. of John Knowe, of Ford, who m. 1711, as his 1st wife,
Philip Bartholomew, of Oxenhoath, and was bur. 9 Mar. 1722.
(Sources, as 3.)

6. Dexter background black
Qly, 1st and 4th, Bartholomew, 2nd, Miller, 3rd, Borlase, impaling, two
coats per fess: in chief, Knowe, and in base, Argent a fess dancetty
sable between three choughs proper (Thomas)
Crest and mantling: As 3.   Motto: Mors janua vitæ

For Philip Bartholomew, of Oxenhoath, who m. 1st, 1711, Mary,
only dau. of John Knowe, and 2nd, Mary, dau. of Alexander Thomas,
of Lamberhurst, and d. 9 Jan. 1730.   (Sources, as 3.)

7. All black background
Qly, 1st and 4th, Bartholomew, 2nd and 3rd, Argent on a bend sable
three trefoils slipped argent (Knowe)
Crest and mantling: As 3.   Motto: In coelo quies   Skull in base
Probably for John Knowe Bartholomew, of Oxenhoath, who d. 1747.
(Sources, as 3.)

8. All black background
Bartholomew arms only
Crest: A demi-goat rampant argent   Mantling and motto: As 7.
Skull in base
Probably for Leonard Bartholomew, who d. 26 Apr. 1757.
(Sources, as 3.)

9. Dexter background black
Qly, 1st, Gules two bars or charged with three mascles two and one
azure, on a canton argent an anchor erect with cable sable (Geary),
2nd, Or two chevronels between three fleurs-de-lys and a bordure
gules (Barber), 3rd, Bartholomew, 4th, Ermine a fess gules between
three wolves' heads erased azure langued gules (Miller), in sinister
chief of shield the Badge of Ulster   In pretence: Qly, 1st and 4th,
Gules on a saltire argent a rose gules (Nevill), 2nd, Argent a chevron
between three boars' heads sable langued gules (Jones), 3rd, Sable on a
bend argent three boars' heads sable langued gules (   )
Crest: From a naval coronet or a dexter hand and arm embowed in a
naval uniform proper, supporting a flag argent charged with a cross
couped gules   Mantling: Gules and argent   Motto: Fideli certa
merces
For Sir William Geary, 2nd Bt., who m. 1810, Henrietta, dau. and
co-heir of Richard Nevill, of Furness, co. Kildare, and d. 6 Aug. 1825.
(B.P. 1939 ed.)

RAMSGATE, St Laurence

1. All black background
On a lozenge   Qly, 1st and 4th, Azure three molets argent within a
double tressure flory counterflory or (Murray), 2nd and 3rd, qly i. &
iv. Or a fess chequy argent and azure (Stuart), ii. & iii. Paly of six or
and sable (Strabolgi)   In pretence: Gules three legs in armour
proper spurred and garnished or conjoined at the thigh in triangle
(Isle of Man); impaling, Or a fess chequy argent and azure within a

double tressure flory counterflory gules, over all a bend engrailed
(Stewart)
Countess's coronet   Mantle: Gules and ermine   Supporters:
Dexter, A savage wreathed about the head and loins vert, his feet in
fetters of iron the chain held up by his right hand proper   Sinister,
A lion gules gorged with a collar azure charged with three molets argent
For Charlotte, dau. of Alexander, 6th Earl of Galloway, who m. 1759,
John, 4th Earl of Dunmore, and d. 11 Nov. 1818.   (B.P. 1949 ed.)

2. All black background
On a decorative lozenge   Argent a shakefork between three molets
sable (Conyngham), impaling, Argent two bendlets wavy sable, on a
chief gules three bezants (Clements)
Baroness's coronet   Mantling: Gules and argent   Motto: Over
fork over   Supporters: Dexter, A horse argent, maned and unguled
or, charged on the shoulder with an eagle displayed or   Sinister, A
buck proper, attired and unguled or, charged on the shoulder with
a griffin's head erased or langued gules
For Elizabeth, eldest dau. of the Rt. Hon. Nathaniel Clements, who m.
1750, Francis, 2nd Baron Conyngham, and d. 31 Oct. 1814.
(B.P. 1949 ed.)

3. Dexter background black
Ermine on a cross sable a roundel argent, on a chief sable three
martlets argent (Wilde), impaling, Azure an eagle displayed argent
armed and crowned or (D'Este)
Baron's coronet   Crest: On a mount vert a stag lodged proper
attired argent holding in the mouth a rose gules slipped vert   Motto:
Equabiliter et diligenter   Supporters: Two greyhounds argent
For Thomas, 1st Baron Truro, who m. 2nd, 1845, Augusta Emma
D'Este, dau. of H.R.H. Augustus Frederick, Duke of Sussex, and
d. 11 Nov. 1855.   (B.P. 1875 ed.)

4. Dexter background black
Sable three sickles interwoven a label in chief argent (Sicklemore),
impaling, Sable a fess cotised between three conies argent (Coney)
Crest: A garb or   Mantling: Gules and argent   Motto: Per pari
Skull below
For John Sicklemore, of Wetheringsett, and Debenham, Suffolk, who
m. 1799, Ann, dau. of Robert Cony, of Walpole Hall, Norfolk, and
d. 5 Feb. 1837.   (B.L.G. 2nd ed.)

5. All black background
Chequy or and sable a fess argent (Winter), impaling, Barry of six or
and azure on a chevron gules three estoiles or (Talworth)
Crest: A hind trippant proper, ducally gorged, lined and ringed or
Mantling: Gules and argent   Motto: Resurgam

For Samuel Winter, of Southwood House, who m. Ann Talworth
(d. 1838), and d. c. 1842.   (O.H.S.)

6. Dexter background black
Or a chevron gules between three lions' gambs erect and erased sable
armed gules (Austen)   In pretence: Argent a chevron between
three cocks gules (Cobb)
Crest: From a mural coronet or a stag sejant argent attired or
Mantling: Gules and argent   Motto: Resurgam
For Nathaniel Austen, who m. Sarah (d. 1839), dau. and co-heiress of
Thomas Cobb, of Sadler's Hall, London, and Lichfield, and d. 1818,
aged 73.   (O.H.S.)

7. Dexter background black
Qly, 1st, Argent a fess and in chief three molets sable (Townley), 2nd,
Argent on a bend sable three covered cups argent (Rixton), 3rd,
Argent a chevron engrailed sable, on a chief sable three martlets argent
(Wilde), 4th, Ermine three greyhounds courant in pale sable collared
gules, on a canton gules a lion passant guardant or (Moore), impaling,
Gules a chevron or between three crescents argent (Gostling)
Crest: A falcon close proper, beaked, perched and belled or, jessed
gules   Mantling: Gules and argent   Motto: Resurgam
For James Townley, of Townley House, and Townley Castle,
Ramsgate, who m. Mary Gostling, and d. 31 Jan. 1817.   (O.H.S.)

8. Dexter background black
Argent a lion passant between two flaunches sable, in chief a label
sable for difference (Garrett), impaling, Argent in chief an eagle
displayed sable crowned or and in base on a mount vert a fox in full
cry reguardant proper (? Ranier)
Crest: A lion passant proper resting dexter paw on a fleur-de-lys or
Mantling: Gules and argent   Motto: Resurgam   In base a skull or
winged gules   Cherub's head at each top corner of shield
For Mark Sellers Garrett, of Nethercourt, who m. Ann Ranier, and
d. 1779, aged 61.   (O.H.S.)

9. Dexter background black
Qly, 1st, Argent on a pile azure three dexter hands couped at the wrist
two and one argent (Jolliffe), 2nd, Argent two bars azure (Hylton),
3rd, Gules six annulets, three, two and one or (Musgrave), 4th, Argent
an inescutcheon gules within an orle of ten molets azure (   ),
impaling, Argent a lion rampant azure armed and langued gules within
a double tressure flory counterflory gules (Lyon)
Crest: Dexter, A cubit arm erect couped vested or holding a broadsword
argent hilted or   Sinister, A bearded human face affronté proper
Motto: Tant que je puis
For Charles Jolliffe, of Southwood House, who d.   (O.H.S.)

10. All black background
Argent on a chevron gules between three lions' heads erased sable
crowned or three bezants (Pettit)
Crest: A lion's gamb erect and erased or holding a roundel sable
Mantling: Gules and argent   On motto scroll: John Gent Pettit
For Capt. John Pettit, who d.   (O.H.S.)

11. All black background
Argent a fess engrailed and in chief three lions rampant gules (   )
Crest: A lion's head affronté erased proper collared or   Mantling:
Gules and argent   Motto: Resurgam   To dexter of shield union
flag, and to sinister red ensign
Unidentified

RIPPLE

1. Dexter background black
Barry of six sable and argent a horse's head erased between three
crescents or, in chief a crescent argent for difference (Sladen),
impaling, Qly, 1st and 4th, Chequy argent and sable (St Barbe), 2nd
and 3rd, Gules a bend between six cross crosslets or (Furneaux)
Crest: On a mount vert a lion's gamb erased sable between two palm
branches proper holding a plume of five feathers gules   Mantling:
Gules and argent   Motto: Vive ut vivas
For John Baker Sladen, of Ripple Court, J.P., D.L., who m. Etheldred,
dau. of Kingsman Baskett St Barbe, and d. 31 Oct. 1860, aged 80.
She d. 28 Sept. 1867, aged 82.   (M.I.)

RIVERHEAD

1. Dexter background black
Gules three tilting spears erect or (Amherst)
Baron's coronet   Crest: On a mount vert three tilting spears or
points upwards one in pale and two in saltire entwined by a wreath of
laurel proper   Supporters: Two Canadian War Indians of a copper
colour, rings in nose and ears and bracelet on arms and wrists argent,
over shoulders two buff belts in saltire, suspended from one a powder
horn, from the other a scalping knife. Before them short aprons azure
tied round the waist with belts gules fimbriated or, gaiters azure
edged top and bottom or, ankles fettered together and chains fixed to
bracelets on exterior wrists proper   Dexter supporter holding
with exterior arm an axe proper   Sinister supporter holding with
exterior arm a tomahawk thereon a scalp proper

Motto: Constantia et virtute
For Jeffery, 1st Baron Amherst, K.B., Field Marshal in the Army,
who d.s.p. 3 Aug. 1797.   (B.P. 1949 ed.)

2. Sinister background black
Two shields   Dexter, within the Order of Hanover, Qly, 1st and 4th,
Gules three tilting spears or headed argent (Amherst), 2nd, Argent on
a fess vert three crosses formy or (Kirby), 3rd, Paly of six or and gules
on a chief gules three escallops or (   )   Sinister, within an
ornamental wreath, Qly as dexter, with in pretence, Azure three arrows
reversed or (Archer)
Countess's coronet   Supporters: As 1.   All on a mantle gules
and ermine
For Sarah, dau. and co-heir of Andrew, 2nd Lord Archer, who m. 1800,
as his 1st wife, William, 1st Earl Amherst, and d. 27 May 1838.
(B.P. 1949 ed.)
(Hatchments of Earl Amherst, and his 2nd wife, are at Knole)

ROLVENDEN

1. Dexter background black
Gules on a fess or between three cushions ermine tasselled or a
fleur-de-lys sable (Hutton), impaling, Qly, 1st and 4th, Vert a dolphin
naiant or (Monypenny), 2nd and 3rd, Azure three cross crosslets
fitchy issuing from three crescents or (Cathcart)
Crest: A Moor, wreathed about the loins, the head adorned with
branches, in the dexter hand a branch proper   Mantling: Gules and
argent   Motto: Resurgam
For the Rev. John Hutton, who m. Silvestra, dau. of James Monypenny,
of Maythorn Hall, and d. 17 Feb. 1828.   (P.R.; Toke MS)

2. All black background
On a lozenge surmounted by a cherub's head
Hutton, impaling, Qly, 1st and 4th, Monypenny, 2nd, Cathcart, 3rd,
Azure three pallets argent, on a chief gules a lion passant guardant or,
all within a bordure ermine (Blackwell)
For Silvestra, widow of the Rev. John Hutton, bur. 3 Aug. 1835.
(P.R.; Toke MS)

3. All black background
Qly, 1st and 4th, Sable two chevrons between three roses argent
barbed vert (Weller), 2nd and 3rd, Azure on a bend engrailed
or three martlets gules (Dawson)
Crest: A greyhound's head erased sable langued gules, holding in the
mouth a rose slipped gules barbed vert   Mantling: Gules and argent

Motto: Steady

For Robert Weller, of Kingsgate House, Rolvenden, bur. 21 May 1839. (P.R.)

ST NICHOLAS-AT-WADE

1. Dexter background black

Argent on a cross sable a leopard's face or (Bridges), impaling, Argent two flaunches sable each charged with a leopard's face or (Denne)

Crest: A man in profile proper couped below the shoulders, vested paly of six argent semy of roundels gules and gules, and wreathed at the temples argent and azure   Mantling: Gules and argent   Motto: In coelo quies   Skull in base

For John Bridges, of St Nicholas Court, who m. Elizabeth, eldest dau. of Thomas Denne, of Monkton Court, and d. 7 Apr. 1823, aged 63. (M.I.)

2. All black background

On a lozenge surmounted by a cherub's head

Arms: As 1.

Skull in base

For Elizabeth, widow of John Bridges, d. 20 Oct. 1841, aged 78.   (M.I.)

ST PAUL'S CRAY, St Paulinus

1. Sinister background black

Sable a cinquefoil between eight cross crosslets or, on a canton or a portcullis sable (Best), impaling, Or a lion passant and in chief three esquires' helmets sable (Knapp)

Baroness's coronet   Motto: Libertas in legibus   Supporters: Two eagles reguardant sable standing on a Roman fasces proper

For Mary Anne, dau. of Jerome Knapp, who m. 1794, William Draper Best, cr. Baron Wynford, 1829, and d. 5 Mar. 1840.   (B.P. 1963 ed.)

2. All black background

Arms: As dexter of 1.

Baron's coronet   Crest: From a ducal coronet or a demi-ostrich rising argent in its beak a cross crosslet fitchy or   Motto and supporters: As 1.

For William, 1st Baron Wynford, d. 3 Mar. 1845.   (B.P. 1963 ed.)

3. All black background

Per chevron argent and gules a crescent counterchanged (Chapman),

impaling, Sable two bars ermine between six martlets, two, two and
two or (Mawe)
Crest: A dexter arm in armour holding a broken tilting spear enfiled
with a chaplet proper   Mantling: Gules and argent
Motto: Resurgam
For James Chapman, who m. Jane, dau. of the Rev. Prebendary Mawe,
and d. 1 Feb. 1824, aged 94.   (Burke's Family Records)

4. Sinister background black
Arms: As 3.
Motto: Resurgam   Two cherubs' heads above shield
For Jane, wife of Jane Chapman. She d. 1820.   (Source, as 3.)

5. All black background
Chapman, impaling, Sable a chevron ermine between three saltires
argent (Greenwood)
Crest, mantling and motto: As 3.
For James Chapman, who m. Mary, dau. of William Greenwood, and
d. 15 Dec. 1845.   (Source, as 3.)

6. Sinister background black
Arms: As 5.
Motto: Resurgam   Two cherubs' heads above shield
For Mary, wife of James Chapman. She d. 1837.   (Source, as 3.)

7. Dexter background black
Chapman, impaling, Per pale gules and azure crusilly or a lion rampant
argent (Hutchinson)
Crest (no helm): As 3, but spear bears pennon with motto, A cuspide
corona   Motto: Resurgam
For James Chapman, who m. Ellen, dau. of the Rev. George
Hutchinson, and d.s.p. 1878.   (Source, as 3.)

8. All black background
Chapman, impaling, Qly, 1st, Sable a unicorn salient argent, armed,
maned and unguled or, within a bordure or (Hay), 2nd, Argent a lion's
head erased within a double tressure flory counterflory gules
(Drummond), 3rd, Argent three escutcheons gules (Hay), 4th, Argent
three bars gules, over all a sword sable hilt and pommel or (Drummond),
the whole impalement within a bordure gules
Crest (no helm): As 3.   Motto (below shield): A cuspide corona
For William Greenwood Chapman, who m. 1840, Elizabeth Catherine,
dau. of Edward William Auriol Drummond-Hay, and d. 23 June 1844.
(Source, as 3.)

(Many of these hatchments were probably destroyed in the fire of 9
Sept. 1968. Only one is known to survive, No. 3; it is still in the church
and in need of attention. The church has been made redundant and is
now in the care of Bromley Age Concern)

SANDWICH, St Clement

1. Sinister background black

Qly, 1st and 4th, Argent on a chevron sable three horseshoes or (Crispe),
2nd and 3rd, Argent a chevron between three oakleaves vert (Tomlin),
impaling, Gules a chevron between three griffins' heads erased or, on a
chief or a lion passant between two annulets gules (Gedding)
Mantling: Gules and argent   Cherub's head above shield
For the 1st wife of Friend Tomlin, who d.   He m. 2nd, Margaret
Norton (d. 1827), and d. 1819.   (M.I. in Fordwich church)

St Mary

1. All black background

Argent on a pale sable three crescents argent (Hayward), impaling,
Azure a lion rampant or armed and langued gules, on a chief or a molet
between two roundels gules (Verrier)
Crest: A wing argent charged with a pale sable thereon three crescents
argent   Mantling: Sable and or   Motto: Mors janua vitæ
For Gervas Hayward, who m. Mary (d. 24 Oct. 1750), dau. of John
Verrier, and d. 16 Oct. 1770.   (M.I.)

2. All black background

On a lozenge   Argent a lion rampant gules armed and langued sable
over all a bend embattled counterembattled or (Stewart), impaling,
Qly, 1st and 4th, Gyronny of eight sable and or (Campbell), 2nd,
Argent a lymphad sable (Lorne), 3rd, Argent a fess chequy or and
sable (Stewart)   Motto: Requiescat in pace   Cherub's head
above and at each side, and winged skull below
For Sarah (Campbell), who m. Joseph Stewart, and d. 11 Mar. 1836,
aged 61. He d. 27 Jan. 1828, aged 66.   (M.I.)

3. All black background

Azure in chief two lions passant in pale or langued gules, in base four
barrulets or (Ranier)
Crest: A lion's head erased argent langued gules semy of roundels
sable and charged on the neck with three fleurs-de-lys two and one
azure, in the mouth a slip of oak proper   Mantling: Gules and
argent   Motto: Non omnis moriar
Probably for Admiral John Spratt Rainier, d. 1822, or Capt. Peter
Rainier, d. 1826.   (M.I.s)

4. All black background

Azure in chief two lions passant in pale and in base four barrulets or
(Rainier)

Crest: A lion's head proper   Mantling: Gules and argent
Motto: Resurgam   Flags crossed in saltire behind shield
For Peter Rainier, Admiral of the Blue, d. 7 Apr. 1808, aged 66.
(M.I.)

St Peter

1. Sinister background black
On a lozenge surmounted by a cherub's head
Two coats per fess, in chief, Gules three fleurs-de-lys one and two
or (Wodsworth), in base, Or a lion rampant gules (   ), impaling,
Paly of six argent and sable, on a chief gules three boars' heads
couped or (Swinford)
Probably for Frances, wife of the Rev. Wm. Wodsworth. She d. 1813.
(M.I.)

Guildhall

1. All black background
Or a lion rampant gules charged on the neck with three chevrons argent
(Rand), impaling, Argent a cross flory between four dogs' heads erased
sable (   )
Crest: Out of a ducal coronet or a boar's head couped sable langued
gules   Mantling: Gules and argent   Motto: Et potents et nobilis
For Capt. Andrew Rand, d. 3 July 1680.
(M.I. in St Mary's Church, Ripple)

SEVENOAKS

1. Dexter background black
Qly, 1st and 4th, Argent a chevron between three weels sable in chief
a label sable (Willard), 2nd, Per bend sinister ermine and sable ermined
argent a lion rampant reguardant or ermined sable, on a chief azure
three estoiles of six points argent (Davis), 3rd, Gules on a bend
sinister argent three eagles displayed sable langued gules (Southern)
Crests: Dexter, A griffin's head erased sable beaked or   Sinister: A
demi-wolf rampant reguardant sable ducally gorged and chained or,
holding in the paws an estoile of six points sable   Mantling: Gules
and argent   Motto: In Domine confido
For Charles Willard, who d. 10 May 1843, aged 81. His wife, Ann, d.
22 Jan. 1868, aged 85.
(M.I. in church; according to B.L.G. 2nd ed. he m. Sarah Lindfield)

2. Dexter background black

On dexter side of hatchment two cartouches   Dexter, within the
Order of the Bath, Argent a bend sable and in sinister chief a garb
gules (Whitworth)   Sinister, within an ornamental wreath,
Whitworth, with in pretence, Argent on a chevron azure between
three roses gules slipped and barbed proper three fleurs-de-lys or, a
crescent sable for difference (Cope)
Earl's coronet   Motto: Dum spiro spero   Supporters: Two
eagles with wings elevated sable beaked and armed or, ducally gorged
or pendant therefrom an escutcheon 'Argent a garb gules'
On sinister side of hatchment   On a lozenge, surmounted by a duke's
coronet, Qly argent and gules a bend vair (Sackville)   In pretence:
Cope   Supporters: Two leopards proper spotted sable   All on a
mantle gules and ermine
Crest: (above and between both achievements) From a ducal coronet
or a garb gules   Inscribed on base of frame: Earl Whitworth
obiit AD 1825.
For Charles, Earl Whitworth, who m. 1801, Arabella Diana, dau. and
co-heir of Sir Charles Cope, 2nd Bt., and widow of John Frederick,
3rd Duke of Dorset, and d. 13 May 1825, aged 71.   (B.E.P.)
(The hatchment of the 3rd Duke of Dorset is in Withyham church,
Sussex)

SHELDWICH

1. All black background

Qly, 1st and 4th, Argent on a chevron engrailed azure between three
martlets sable three crescents or (Watson), 2nd and 3rd, Or two
chevrons gules (Monson)
Baron's coronet   Crest: A griffin's head erased ducally gorged argent
Motto: Esto quod esse videris   Supporters: Dexter, A griffin argent
ducally gorged or   Sinister, A bear proper gorged with a belt,
buckled, the strap pendent argent, charged with two crescents or
For Lewis Richard, 3rd Baron Sondes, who d. unm. 14 Mar. 1836.
(B.P. 1963 ed.)

2. Dexter background black

Ermine a millrind between two martlets in pale sable, on a chief
engrailed azure two wings conjoined and expanded or (Milles),
impaling, Azure three cross crosslets fitchy between two bendlets or
(Knatchbull)
Baron's coronet   Crest: A lion rampant or ermined sable
Motto: Esto quod esse videris   Supporters: As 1.
For George John, 4th Baron Sondes, who m. 1823, Eleanor, 5th dau. of
Sir Edward Knatchbull, 8th Bt., and d. 17 Dec. 1874.   (Source, as 1.)

SHOREHAM

1. All black background
Argent on a chevron azure three fishes hauriant argent (?Pennell)
Crest: A dexter mailed arm embowed holding a scimitar all proper
Mantling: Gules and argent   Motto: Resurgam
Unidentified
(In need of repair and removed temporarily from the church)

SUNDRIDGE

1. All black background
Or ermined sable a saltire azure between two thistles in pale proper and
two molets in fess azure (Grasett), impaling, Sable two swords in saltire
argent pommels and hilts or between four fleurs-de-lys or (Barrow)
Crest: Between two branches of palm proper a bent bow in pale the
arrow point to the dexter or   Mantling: Gules and argent
Motto: Resurgam
For William Grassett, of Ovenden House, Sundridge, who m. 2nd,
Eliza, dau. of Henry Barrow, of Hill Park, Kent, and d. 18 Apr. 1841.
(card in church)

2. Dexter background black
Or two fleurs-de-lys bendwise sable between two bendlets azure
(D'Oyly), impaling, Vert two bendlets wavy ermine on a canton or
five roundels gules (Bruere)
Crest: A demi-dragon proper   Mantling: Gules and argent
Motto: Omne solum forti patria
For the Rev. George D'Oyly, D.D., Rector of Sundridge, who m.
Maria Frances dau. of William Bruere, and d. 1846.
(B.E.B.; card in church)

3. All black background
Gules a dove volant argent beaked or with an olive branch vert in the
beak, perched on two snakes entwined chainwise and in chevron
proper, with a crescent argent for difference in centre chief (Sloper),
impaling, Qly, 1st and 4th, Argent a chevron between three estoiles
sable (Mordaunt), 2nd and 3rd, Lozengy argent and sable (Shipley)
Crest: On two snakes entwined chainwise proper a dove volant argent
beaked or, with an olive branch vert in its beak   Mantling: Gules
and argent   Motto: Resurgam
For William Charles Sloper, who m. Amelia, dau. of the Rev. Jonathan
Shipley, D.D., Bishop of St Asaph, by Anna Maria, dau. and co-heiress
of the Hon. and Rev. George Mordaunt, and was buried at Sundridge,
20 Mar. 1844.   (card in church)

4. All black background
On a lozenge surrounded by ornamental scrollwork
Gules a lion rampant argent a chief chequy or and azure (Warren),
impaling, Sloper without crescent
For Amelia Sloper, who m. Charles Warren, Chief Justice of Chester,
and d. 1845. He d. 1829.   (O.H.S.)

5. All black background
Argent a buck's head cabossed sable between the attires a cross sable
(Vyse)
Motto: Resurgam   Shield is surmounted by a cherub's head issuing
from clouds, and flanked by two branches
For the Rev. William Vyse, LL.D., Rector of Sundridge, 1777–1816,
d. 10 Feb. 1816, aged 75.   (card in church)

SUTTON-AT-HONE

1. Sinister background black
Argent a chevron gules between three parrots' heads couped vert
beaked gules (Lethieullier), impaling, Gules a chevron between ten
crosses formy six and four argent (Berkeley)
Motto: In coelo quies   Cherub's head above shield
For Mary Berkeley, who m. as his 1st wife, John Lethieullier, and was
bur. 29 June 1784.   (P.R.; O.H.S.)

2. Dexter background black
Lethieullier, as 1, impaling, Argent on a fess sable a lion passant argent
(Garrard)
Crest: A parrot proper   Mantling: Gules and argent   Motto:
Omne solum forte patria   Skull in base
For John Lethieullier, who m. 1st, Mary Berkeley, and 2nd, Anne
Garrard, and d. 3 May 1760.   (P.R.; O.H.S.)

3. All black background
On a lozenge surmounted by a cherub's head
Argent a chevron gules between three parrots vert beaked gules
(Lethieullier)   In pretence: Argent on a fess sable a lion statant
argent (Garrard)
For Ann, widow of John Lethieullier, bur. 10 Dec. 1772.
(P.R.; O.H.S.)

4. Dexter background black
Argent a lion rampant between eight cross crosslets sable (Mumford),
impaling, Per chevron argent and gules a crescent counterchanged
(Chapman)

Crest: From a ducal coronet or a talbot's head sable   Mantling:
Gules and argent   Motto: Resurgam
For John Mumford, of St John's, who m. 1st, Elizabeth, dau. of John
Nash, M.D., of Sevenoaks, and 2nd, Elizabeth, dau. of Mr. Serjeant
Leigh, of Howley, and 3rd, Anne Eleanor, 2nd dau. of James Chapman,
of Pauls Cray Hill, and d. 23 Aug. 1825, aged 73.
(M.I.; Surrey Arch. Colls.)

5. Sinister background black
Mumford, impaling, Gules on a chevron sable three lions rampant
argent, in centre chief an annulet sable for cadency (Leigh)
Motto: Resurgam   Cherub's head at each top corner of shield,
which is suspended from decorative green ribbons
For Elizabeth, dau. of Mr. Serjeant Leigh, 2nd wife of John Mumford,
d.   (O.H.S.)

6. Dexter background black
Argent a lion rampant azure between eight cross crosslets gules
(Mumford), impaling, Azure on a bend wavy or between two dolphins
naiant embowed argent three escallops gules (Fleet)
Crest: A talbot's head erased sable, eared and ducally gorged or langued
gules   Mantling: Gules and argent   Motto: Resurgam
For William Mumford, of Sutton Place, who m. Mary Fleet, and d.
1821.   (O.H.S.)

7. All black background
On a lozenge surmounted by a cherub's head
Argent a lion rampant sable between eight cross crosslets gules
(Mumford), impaling, Fleet
Motto: Resurgam
For Mary, widow of William Mumford, d. 1831.   (O.H.S.)

8. Sinister background black
Or on a chevron sable three lions rampant argent (Leigh)
In pretence: Qly, 1st and 4th, Sable a shinbone in fess surmounted by
another in pale argent (Baynes), 2nd and 3rd, Argent two bends wavy
sable, on a chief azure three annulets or (   )
Motto: In coelo quies   Cherub's head above shield
For Lucy Baines, who m. Francis Leigh, and was bur. 3 Sept. 1764.
(Surrey Arch. Colls, Vol. 7)

9. All black background
On a lozenge surmounted by a cherub's head
Leigh, as 8, impaling, Sable three lions passant in bend between four
bendlets argent (Browne)
Motto: Resurgam
For Elizabeth, dau. of Prosper Browne, of Dartford, who m. Richard
Leigh, Serjeant at Law, and d. 1811.   (Sources, as 8.)

10. Sinister background black

Leigh, as 8, in dexter chief an annulet sable for difference, impaling,
Argent a lion rampant between eight cross crosslets sable (Mumford)
Motto: Resurgam   Cherub's head at each top corner of shield,
which is suspended by ribbons
For Elizabeth Mumford, who m. Richard Leigh, son of Richard Leigh,
Serjeant-at-Law, and d. 1810.   (Sources, as 8.)

11. All black background

Arms. As 10.
Crest: On a mount vert a lion sejant guardant argent charged on the
breast with an annulet sable   Mantling: Gules and argent
Motto: Resurgam
For Richard Leigh, who d. 1828, aged 67.   (Sources, as 8.)
(This hatchment was in poor condition when recorded in 1955, and is
now missing)

12. Dexter background black

Qly of nine, 1st, Leigh, as 8, 2nd, Azure on a chief indented argent
three pierced molets azure (Coppendale), 3rd, Gules on a bend argent
three cross crosslets fitchy sable (   ), 4th, Sable a lion rampant or
a bordure compony sable and or (   ), 5th, Or three stags' heads
cabossed sable (   ), 6th, Per pale and per chevron or and sable
three greyhounds heads erased counterchanged (Olyff), 7th, Argent a
chevron between three squirrels gules (Lovell), 8th, Gules a lion passant
guardant in chief three stirrups or (Gifford), 9th, Browne, as 9, impaling,
Argent an eagle displayed sable on a chief sable three crescents
argent (Moon)
Crest: As 11.   Motto: In coelo quies
For Richard Leigh, who m. Jane Moon, and d. 9 Oct. 1841, aged 59.
(Sources, as 8.)

13. Dexter background black

Qly, 1st and 4th, Gyronny of eight or and sable (Campbell), 2nd and
3rd, Argent a lymphad sable pennants gules (Lorne), impaling,
Gules an eagle displayed or crowned and taloned argent within an orle
of eight cross crosslets or (Graves)
Crest: A dexter cubit arm the hand proper holding a spur in fess rowel
to sinister or   Mantling: Gules and argent   Motto: Resurgam
For Momford Campbell, who m. Frances Sarah Graves, and d. 1856.
(O.H.S.)

TESTON

1. All black background

Argent on a chief sable three covered cups or in centre chief the Badge

of Ulster (Boteler)   In pretence: Qly, 1st, Argent a chevron between
three cocks gules, on a chief sable three spearheads argent (Williams),
2nd, Argent a greyhound courant sable (Williams), 3rd, Argent a cross
chequy azure and or (   ), 4th, Per chevron sable and argent three
elephants' heads erased counterchanged (Sanders)
Crest: Two eagles (supporting a vine) proper   Mantling: Gules and
argent   Motto: Aquilæ vitem pocula vitam
For Sir Philip Boteler, 3rd Bt., of Teston, who m. Elizabeth, only dau.
and heir of Thomas Williams, of Cabalva, Radnor, and d. 22 Jan.
1772.   (B.E.B.)

2. All black background
On a lozenge surmounted by two cherubs' heads
Sable on a chevron or between three boars passant argent langued
gules three falcons' heads erased sable langued and armed gules
(Iremonger), impaling, Ermine a fess wavy azure between three choughs
proper (Gambier)
For Harriet, sister of James, Lord Gambier, who m. as his 2nd wife,
the Rev. Lascelles Iremonger, and d. 8 Oct. 1834.
(B.L.G. 7th ed.; P.R.)

3. All black background
Per fess or and gules a lion rampant within a double tressure flory
counterflory all counterchanged, in centre chief the Badge of
Ulster (Middleton), impaling, Sable three covered cups or (   )
Baron's coronet   Crest: From a tower sable a demi-lion rampant
gules langued sable holding in the paws an anchor erect sable
Mantle: Gules edged or   Motto: In coelo quies   Supporters:
Dexter, An angel proper vested argent, mantled purpure, belted, wings
elevated, with a celestial crown or, in her exterior hand a sword erect
proper pommelled and hilted or   Sinister, A sea-horse argent
maned or langued gules, gorged with a naval crown azure, in the mouth
a thistle proper   Winged skull in base
For Charles, 1st Baron Barham, Admiral of the Red, who m. 1761,
Margaret (d. 10 Oct. 1792), dau. of James Gambier, and d. 17 June
1813.   (B.P. 1949 ed.)

4. Sinister background black
Qly, 1st and 4th, Or fretty gules a canton ermine (Noel), 2nd and 3rd,
Gules a lion rampant argent (   ), impaling, Gules a lion rampant
argent langued gules a bordure engrailed argent (Grey)
Mantling: Gules and argent   Motto: In coelo quies   Cherub's
head above
For Elizabeth, dau. of the Hon. Sir George Grey, 1st Bt., who m.
1817, as his 2nd wife, Charles Noel (later 1st Earl of Gainsborough),
and d. 20 Sept. 1818.   (B.P. 1949 ed.)

5. Sinister background black

Qly, 1st and 4th, Per fess or and gules a lion rampant counterchanged
(Middleton), 2nd and 3rd, Noel, impaling, Qly, 1st and 4th, Argent a
lion rampant gules (   ), 2nd and 3rd, Gules a lion rampant
sable (   )
Baroness's coronet   Motto: In coelo quies   Supporters: Two
eagles sable langued and clawed gules each charged on the breast with
an anchor between cords or   Winged skull in base
Presumably for Arabella, 2nd dau. of Sir James Hamlyn-Williams, Bt.,
who m. 1820, as his 3rd wife, Charles Noel (who succeeded as 3rd
Lord Barham 1823), and d. 4 Oct. 1829.   (B.P. 1963 ed.)

6. Dexter background black

Qly, 1st and 4th Noel, 2nd, Middleton, as 3, but no Badge of Ulster,
3rd, Per fess or and azure a lion rampant per fess gules and or langued
azure within a tressure flory counterflory counterchanged (Middleton),
over all the Badge or Ulster, impaling, Azure a circular wreath argent
and azure with four hawks' bells conjoined thereto in quadrangle
or (Jocelyn)
Earl's coronet   Crest: A buck statant argent attired and unguled or
Motto: Tout bien ou rien   Supporters: Two bulls argent langued
gules navally gorged azure therefrom a chain reflexed over the back or,
pendent from the crown an escutcheon azure charged with an anchor
encircled by a wreath of laurel or
For Charles Noel, 1st Earl of Gainsborough, who m. 4th, 1833,
Frances (d. 12 May 1885), dau. of Robert, 3rd Earl of Roden, and d.
10 June 1866.   (B.P. 1949 ed.)

THROWLEY

1. All black background

Two cartouches   Dexter, within the circlet and collar of the Star of
India, Vert on a chevron embattled or ermined sable between three
hedgehogs or three bombs sable fired proper, upon a chief of
Augmentation, the gates and fortress of Seringapatam, the drawbridge
let down, and the Union flag hoisted over the flag of Tippoo, all
proper (Harris)   Sinister, within an ornamental border, as dexter,
impaling, Azure three garbs or (Commins)
Baron's coronet   Crest: On a mural coronet or a Bengal tiger
passant guardant vert striped or, pierced in the breast with an arrow
and crowned with an Eastern crown or   Mantling (slight): Vert and
or   Motto: My prince and my country   Supporters: Dexter, A
Grenadier proper in his exterior hand a staff, thereon the Union flag
over the standard of Tippoo Sultan   Sinister, A Malay soldier
proper holding a like staff, thereon the flag of the East India Company

over the standard of Tippoo; in each instance the tricolour is furled
at the base of the staff, the dexter inscribed 'Republique' and the
sinister 'Francaise'
For George Francis Robert, 3rd Baron Harris, G.C.S.I., who m. 1850,
Sarah (d. 6 Mar. 1853), dau. of the Ven. George Cummins, Archdeacon
of Trinidad, and d. 23 Nov. 1872.   (B.P. 1949 ed.)

TONBRIDGE

1. Dexter background black
Or a saltire engrailed gules (Children), impaling, Sable two chevrons
between three roses argent (Weller)
Crest: A horse's head erased argent   Mantling: Gules and argent
Motto: Spe vitæ morior   Cherubs' heads at top corners of shield and
skull below
For John Children, who m. Jane, dau. of Robert Weller, and d. 27
Apr. 1770.   (M.I.)

2. All black background
On a lozenge surmounted by a cherub's head
Arms: As 1.
Motto: In spe quiesco   Skull below
For Jane, widow of John Children, d. 6 Feb. 1789.   (M.I.)

3. All black background
On a lozenge surmounted by a cherub's head
Or a fess between six lions' heads erased gules (Goodwyn), impaling,
Vert a saltire between four eagles displayed or (Leigh)
For Mary, widow of John Groombridge, who m. Henry Goodwyn,
of Barn Hill, Haysden, and d. 30 Nov. 1816.   (M.I.)

4. Dexter background black
Argent on a chevron gules between three bears' gambs erased and erect
sable three crescents or (Harvey), impaling, Sable a fess or between
three cinquefoils argent (Davis)
Crest: Two bears' gambs erect and erased sable holding between them
a crescent or   Mantling: Gules and argent   Motto: Spero meliora
Skull in base
For Thomas Harvey, of Tonbridge, who m. Charlotte, dau. of the Rev.
William Davis, and d. 9 June 1779.   (M.I. in churchyard)

5. Dexter background black
Argent three horses rampant sable langued gules (Hickeringill)
In pretence, and impaling, Qly, 1st and 4th, Ermine a cross potent
azure (Leming), 2nd and 3rd, Argent three bulls' heads erased sable
(Skeffington)

Crest: A moor's head proper, wreathed at the temples or and azure, and adorned with a pearl earring   Mantling: Gules and argent
Motto: Resurgam
For Mathias Hickeringill, who m. Mrs. Elizabeth Leming, née Skeffington, and d. 10 Nov. 1742.   (A.C. Vol. X, 39–45)

6. Sinister background black
Qly, 1st and 4th, Gules a falcon volant within an orle engrailed argent (Knox), 2nd and 3rd, Ermine a chevron between three wolves' heads erased vert langued gules (   ), impaling, Paly of six or and vert on a chief vert three crosses formy or (Meux)
Cherub's head at each upper angle of shield
For Fanny, dau. of Richard Meux, who m. 1815, Vicesimus Knox, and d.   (B.P. 1868 ed.)

7. Dexter background black
Argent a chevron gules between three pheons reversed sable (Sulyard)
In pretence: Argent a chevron between three hawks' heads erased sable langued gules (Honywood)
Crest: A buck's head couped proper   Mantling: Gules and argent
Motto: Resurgam
Unidentified

8. All black background
Qly, 1st and 4th, Argent on a chevron sable between three squirrels sejant each holding a nut proper three acorns or (Woodgate), 2nd and 3rd, Sable a fess embattled or ermined sable between three dexter gauntlets or (Birsty), impaling, Gules a lion rampant between three escallops or (Ponton)
Crest: A squirrel sejant holding a nut proper   Mantling: Gules and or   Motto: Gloria et Deo
For Francis Woodgate, of Ferox Hall, Tonbridge, who m. Martha Ponton, of Nizells, Hildenborough, and d. 13 May, 1843. She d. 1842. (M.I. in churchyard)

TUNSTALL

1. Dexter background black
Qly, 1st and 4th, Sable a fess engrailed argent in chief a molet between two crosses formy fitchy argent (Bradley), 2nd and 3rd, Azure on a chevron or three cinquefoils gules a canton ermine (Hawes)   In pretence: Bradley
Crest: A dexter arm embowed in armour holding a battleaxe proper
Mantling: Gules and argent   Motto: Requiescat in pace

For Andrew Hawes Dyne, who m. 1783, Frances, sister and heir of
James Bradley, took by sign-manual in 1800 the surname of Bradley,
and d. 5 Dec. 1820.   (B.L.G. 2nd ed.; M.I. in church)

2. All black background

Gules three arrows in pale two and one points downwards argent,
feathered argent and barbed or, in chief the Badge of Ulster (Hales),
impaling to the dexter, Argent a cross between four crosses formy
fitchy gules (Bealing), and to the sinister, Ermine two bars or over all a
lion rampant azure (Bagnall)
Crest: A dexter arm embowed at the elbow proper garnished or and
bound with a ribbon gules holding an arrow argent as in the arms,
but fessways the barb to the dexter   Mantling: Gules and argent
Motto: Unum est necesarium
For Sir John Hales, 4th Bt., who m. 1st, Helen, dau. of Sir Richard
Bealing, of Ireland, and 2nd, Helen, dau. of Dudley Bagnel, of
Newry, and d. Jan. 1744.   (B.E.B.)

3. Dexter background black

Gules on a bend or between six roundels argent three roundels gules a
chief or ermined sable (Dixon), impaling, Per pale gules and azure a
tiger passant argent (Mabbe)
Crest: A bear's gamb or ermined sable banded argent
Mantling: Gules and argent
For Robert Dixon, Rector of Tunstall, 1647–76, who m. Sarah,
dau. of Thomas Mabb, and d. May 1688.   (D.N.B.; Visit. Kent)

4. Sinister background black

Dixon, impaling, Gules a chevron ermine on a chief or three
fleurs-de-lys sable (   )
Crest and mantling: As 3.
Possibly for Robert Dixon, son of 3, Rector of Tunstall 1676–1711,
who m. Mrs. Elizabeth Bowles, and d. Mar. 1711.   (Sources, as 3.)

WALDERSHARE

1. Dexter background black

Qly of eight, 1st, Gules three crescents or (Monins), 2nd, Gules
crusilly argent a cross formy argent (   ), 3rd, Ermine on a chief
gules three sinister hands couped at the wrist argent (Malmaison),
4th, Gules a chevron ermine between three squirrels sejant holding
acorns or (Greenford), 5th, Argent a fess gules between three
chessrooks sable (Swanton), 6th Argent on a chevron azure three
leopards' faces or (   ), 7th, Sable a lion rampant langued and
armed gules between three crosses formy or (Ayliffe), 8th, Azure

three lions rampant argent langued and armed gules (   ), in fess
point the Badge of Ulster, impaling, Qly of six, 1st and 6th, Azure
a lion rampant or langued and armed gules ducally crowned
argent (Darell), 2nd, Argent a fess dancetty gules in chief three molets
sable (Barrett), 3rd, Gules a cross crosslet ermine (Norton), 4th, Gules
an eagle displayed argent (Atbridge), 5th, Sable three hunting horns
stringed sable (Horne)
Crest: An increscent or   Mantling: Gules and argent   Motto:
Vivat post funera virtus   Inscribed on frame: Sir Thomas Monins
Bart of Waldershare in the County of Kent dyed the 20th of January
A° Dm, 1677-8
For Sir Thomas Monins, 3rd Bt., who m. Elizabeth, dau. of James
Darell, of Colehill, and d.s.p. 20 Jan. 1678, aged 73.
(B.E.B.)

2. Dexter background black
Qly of 16, 1st, and 16th, Azure a lion passant or between three
fleurs-de-lys argent (North), 2nd, Argent on a bend azure three lions
passant argent langued gules (Dale), 3rd, Sable on a chevron between
three pheons argent three molets gules (   ), 4th, Or a cross flory
sable (Brockett), 5th, Gules on a saltire argent a fleur-de-lys azure
(   ), 6th, Argent a lion rampant azure langued gules (   ),
7th, Or on a pile azure a griffin segreant or (   ), 8th, Gules three
escutcheons argent (   ), 9th, Gules three bars gemel argent
(Bensell), 10th, Argent a fess dancetty gules between three molets
sable (More), 11th, Barry of six ermine and gules in chief a crescent
sable for difference (   ), 12th, Argent three fusils conjoined
in fess gules a bordure sable a molet sable for difference (Montagu),
13th, Per pale or and azure on a chevron between three griffins'
heads erased four fleurs-de-lys all counterchanged (Pope), 14th, Or an
escutcheon within an orle of eight martlets sable (Brownlow), 15th,
Argent two bendlets sable (   ) impaling, Azure a cross
flory or (Warde)
Earl's coronet   Crest: A dragon's head erased sable scaled or,
ducally gorged or   Motto: Animo et fide   Supporters: Two
mastiffs proper
For Francis, 6th Earl of Guilford, who m. 2nd, 1826, Harriet, dau. of
Lt.-Gen. Sir Henry Warde, and d. 29 Jan. 1861.
(B.P. 1949 ed.)

3. Dexter background black
North, impaling, Azure a chevron between three molets or (Chetwynd)
Earl's coronet   Crest: A dragon's head erased sable langued gules,
scaled, ducally gorged and chained or   Motto and supporters: As 2.
For Dudley Francis, 7th Earl of Guilford, who m. 1874, Georgiana,
dau. of Sir George Chetwynd, 3rd Bt., and d. 19 Dec. 1885.
(B.P. 1949 ed.)

WALMER

1. All black background

Two oval shields   Dexter, within the Garter, Qly, 1st and 4th,
Gules a cross argent in each quarter five roundels argent in saltire
(Wellesley), 2nd and 3rd, Or a lion rampant gules langued sable
ducally gorged or (Colley), over all an escutcheon charged with the
Union flag   Sinister, within an ornamental wreath, Qly as dexter,
impaling, Qly, 1st and 4th, Qly or and gules in the first quarter an
eagle displayed vert (Pakenham), 2nd, Argent on a bend wavy between
two bendlets sable each charged with three roundels argent three
fleurs-de-lys argent (Cuff), 3rd, Ermine a griffin segreant azure armed
or (Aungier)

Duke's coronet   Crest: From a ducal coronet or a demi-lion gules
bearing a staff or with a forked pennon flowing to the sinister argent
and gules charged with the cross of St George   Motto: Virtutis
fortuna comes   Supporters: Two lions gules each gorged with an
antique crown and chained or

For Arthur, 1st Duke of Wellington, K.G., who m. 1806, Catherine,
dau. of Edward, 2nd Baron Longford, and d. 14 Sept. 1852.

(B.P. 1949 ed.)

(There is another hatchment for the Duke in the parish church at
Stratfieldsaye in Hampshire)

2. Dexter background black

Two oval shields   Dexter, within Order of the Bath, Azure on a
chevron embattled between in chief two lions' gambs erased erect
and in base an anchor or a bomb sable fired proper between two
crescents sable, on a canton or an olive branch vert (Harvey)
Sinister, as dexter, impaling, Or a griffin segreant sable a bordure
gules (Boys)

Crest: Two lions' gambs erect sable holding a crescent or and
surrounded with a wreath of laurel proper   Motto: Persevere
Supporters: Dexter, A sailor proper in his dexter hand a staff bearing a
flag with a cross gules in the dexter canton a lion's gamb sable
Sinister, A griffin sable navally gorged or   All on a mantle gules
and argent bearing Star of the Bath

For Sir Henry Harvey, K.B., Admiral of the White, who m. Elizabeth
(Boys), and d. 28 Dec. 1810.   (M.I.)

3. All black background

On a curvilinear lozenge

Harvey, impaling, Boys

Supporters and mantle: As 1.   Motto: Resurgam   Cherub's head
above

For Elizabeth, widow of Sir Henry Harvey, d. 7 Mar. 1823.

(M.I.)

4. Dexter background black, including dexter background of sinister shield

Two shields   Dexter, within Order of the Bath, Argent a lion rampant gules langued sable navally crowned azure, on a canton sable a medal or ribboned argent (Lee)   Sinister, within an ornamental wreath, as dexter, impaling, Sable a griffin segreant argent (   )
Crest: A demi-lion or langued gules navally crowned azure holding a sceptre sable headed with a fleur-de-lys or   Motto: Resurgam
Medals and Orders pendent below dexter shield
For Sir Richard Lee, K.C.B., Admiral of the Blue, who m. Elizabeth Honora, and d. 5 Aug. 1807, aged 78. She d. 8 May 1867, aged 92.
(M.I.)

5. Dexter background black

Argent on a chevron between three herons sable three escallops or (Browne), impaling, Qly, 1st and 4th, qly i. & iv. Argent a fess between three crescents gules, ii. & iii. Or an orle azure, on a chief (over both coats) sable six annulets, three, two and one or (Ogle), 2nd and 3rd, Sable a lion passant guardant or between three helms argent garnished or (Compton)
Crest: On a mount vert a coney courant argent   Mantling: Gules and argent   Motto: Peur gagne peu
For Rear-Admiral E. Walpole Browne, who m. 1845, Hannah, dau. of Robert Ogle, of Eglingham, and d. 15 Oct. 1846.
(B.L.G. 5th ed., M.I.)

6. All black background

On a lozenge surmounted by three cherubs' heads
Argent three lions rampant gules langued sable (   ), impaling, Or a fess wavy between three escallops sable (Ladd)
Motto: Resurgam   Skull in base
Unidentified

WATERINGBURY

1. All black background

Argent a fess between six annulets gules (Lucas), impaling, Argent on a chevron engrailed azure between three martlets sable three cinquefoils or (Heyman)
Crest: From a ducal coronet or a demi-dragon gules   Mantling: Gules and argent   Motto: Ne timeas nisi Deum
For Matthias Prime Lucas, Lord Mayor of London, who m. Polly Heyman, and d. 2 Jan. 1848. She d. 1841.
(Pedigree in vestry of church)

2. All black background
On a lozenge surmounted by a gold knot
Qly, 1st, Argent two bars gules, on a canton gules a lion of England
(Lancaster), 2nd, Gules three stags' heads cabossed or (Dering),
3rd, Azure six lions rampant three, two and one argent (Leybourne),
4th, Argent a saltire engrailed sable (Wootton)   In pretence: Argent
a fess between six annulets gules (Lucas)
Motto: In coelo quies
For Mary Frances, dau. of Matthias Prime Lucas, who m. Samuel
Lancaster, and d. 14 Aug. 1858.   (B.L.G. 5th ed.; G.M.)

EAST WICKHAM, St Michael

1. Sinister background black
Qly, 1st and 4th, qly i. & iv. Per bend ermine and sable ermined argent
a lion rampant or langued gules within a bordure engrailed or (Jones),
ii. & iii. Gules a cross crossed on a griece of three steps or (Jones),
2nd and 3rd, qly i. & iv. Azure three pelicans in their piety proper
(Pelham), ii. and iii. Gules two belts palewise argent the buckles in
chief or (Pelham), impaling, Sable a fess between three elephants' heads
erased argent (   )
Motto: In coelo quies   A cherub's head at each top corner of shield
Unidentified.

2. All black background
Qly, as dexter of 1.
To dexter of main shield, Qly as above with in pretence, Or on a
chevron between three lions' heads erased sable three pheons argent
(Hening) S.Bl.   To sinister of main shield, Qly as above, impaling,
Gules a chevron between three garbs or (   ) D. Bl.
Crest: A demi-lion rampant or langued gules, holding in its dexter paw
a cross crosslet fitchy erect sable   Mantling: Gules and argent
Motto: Resurgam
For John Pelham Jones, who m. 1st, Elizabeth Hening, and 2nd,
Catherine Hester, and d.   (P.R.)

WEST WICKHAM

1. All black background
Within the Order of the Bath, with Badge of Order pendent below
Qly, 1st and 4th, Argent a fess dancetty sable (West), 2nd and 3rd,
Sable three leopards' faces jessant-de-lys or (West), impaling, Qly, 1st
and 4th, Ermine three lions passant guardant in pale sable (Adams),

2nd and 3rd, Argent on a pale sable three towers argent (   )
Crest: From a ducal coronet or a griffin's head azure beaked and eared
or   Motto: Jour de ma vie
For Admiral Sir John West, G.C.B., of Braywick Lodge, who m. 1817,
Harriet, dau. of John Adams, of Northampton, and d. 18 Mar. 1862.
(B.L.G. 5th ed.)

2. Dexter background black
Qly, 1st and 4th, Gules three bendlets argent, over all three stags' heads
cabossed or (Beachcroft), 2nd, Sable a lion rampant argent (Mathew),
3rd, Gules a bend or (Porten), impaling, Gules on a fess or between
two chevrons ermine three leopards' faces sable (Seward)
Crest: From six park pales or a beech tree proper   Mantling: Gules
and argent   Motto: Non intemperatus sed firmus
Probably for Samuel Beachcroft, who m. Miss Seward and d. 1784.
(G.M.)

3. All black background
On a lozenge   Arms: As 2, but Beachcroft coat, Bendy of six argent
and gules, etc.
Motto: In coelo quies
Probably for the widow of Samuel Beachcroft. She d. 1803.   (G.M.)

4. Dexter background black
Arms: As 3.
Motto: Resurgam   Cherub's head at each top corner of shield
Probably for Matthews Beachcroft, who m. Miss Seward and d. 1823,
aged 64.   (G.M.)

5. Sinister background black
Vert a lion rampant reguardant crowned between three arrows points
downwards or (Gildart), impaling, Qly, 1st and 4th, Or a cross vert
(Hussey), 2nd and 3rd, Sable a bend between six cross crosslets fitchy
argent(Lake)
Motto: Resurgam   Two cherubs' heads above shield
For Anne Elizabeth Hussey, who m. the Rev. Frederick Gildart, and
and d. 12 Nov. 1817, aged 42.   (M.I.)

6. All black background
Arms: As 5.
Crests: Dexter, A demi-lion rampant reguardant crowned or
Sinister, Six arrows in saltire points downwards or   Mantling:
Gules and argent
For the Rev. Frederick Gildart, who d. 1841, aged 71.   (M.I.)

7. All black background
On a lozenge surmounted by a cherub's head
Qly, 1st, qly i. & iv. Azure on a chevron or between three storks argent

three roses gules barbed vert (Farnaby), ii. & iii. Argent three bars
gemel gules on a bend or a lion passant gules (Lloyd), 2nd, Azure
three chevronels between three molets or (Delafosse), 3rd, qly i.
& iv. Per pale argent and gules a cross engrailed counterchanged in
dexter chief a cinquefoil gules (Lant), ii. & iii. Gules on a saltire
or another couped vert (Andrews), 4th, Azure a lion rampant between
eight cinquefoils or (Loyd), in chief the Badge of Ulster   In
pretence: Or on a fess gules three fleurs-de-lys or (Lennard)
For Mary, only dau. and heir of Samuel Lennard, who m. Sir John
Farnaby, 4th Bt., and d. 9 May 1833, aged 83.
(M.I.; B.P. 1855 ed.)

8. Dexter background black
Qly of six, 1st, qly i. & iv. Farnaby, ii. & iii. Lloyd, 2nd, Delafosse,
3rd, Lennard, 4th, qly i. & iv. Lant, ii. & iii. Andrews, 5th, Loyd,
6th, Delafosse, the Badge of Ulster, impaling, Azure a griffin segreant
or (Morland)
Crest: From a mural coronet or a stork proper charged on the neck
with three bends gules   Mantling: Gules and argent   Motto:
Resurgam
For the Rev. Sir Charles Francis Farnaby, 5th Bt., who m. Elizabeth,
dau. of Thomas Morland, of Lamberhurst, and d. 29 Aug. 1859, aged
71.   (M.I.; B.P. 1855 ed.)

9. All black background
On a lozenge surmounted by a cherub's head
Arms: As 8.
Motto: Resurgam
For Elizabeth, widow of the Rev. Sir Charles Francis Farnaby, 5th
Bt., who d. 25 Aug. 1861, aged 79.   (M.I.; B.P. 1855 ed.)

WILMINGTON

1. Dexter background black
Two oval shields   Dexter, within the Order of Hanover and with
Badge of Order pendent below, Argent three piles one issuing from the
chief between two reversed in base sable, on a canton azure the Prince
of Wales feathers issuing from a mural coronet or (Hulse)   Sinister,
within an ornamental wreath, Hulse, impaling, Azure three oval
buckles tongues to the sinister or (   )
Crest: A buck's head erased proper between the attires a sun or
Mantling: Gules and argent   Motto: Esse quam videri   Supporters:
Two horses rampant reguardant argent collared, maned and tailed or,
and gorged with wreaths of laurel proper; dexter has pendent shield
gules charged with three ostrich feathers issuing from a mural coronet

or, and sinister has pendent shield or charged with a grenade sable
fired or
For Field Marshal Sir Samuel Hulse, K.C.H., who m. Charlotte, and
d.s.p. 1 Jan. 1837.   (B.P. 1963 ed.)
(There is another hatchment for Sir Samuel at Breamore, Hampshire)

WOOLWICH, St Mary

1. All black background
On a lozenge, surmounted by a cherub's head and skull below
Argent a wyvern gules (Drake), impaling, Argent a millrind gules
(Marshall)
Possibly for Isabella, dau. and heiress of Thomas Marshall, who m.
Montagu Garrard Drake, of Shardeloes, M.P. for Amersham, and
d.   He. d. 1728.   (B.L.G. 2nd ed.)

WYE

1. Sinister background black
Qly, 1st and 4th, Or two bars azure each charged with a barrulet
dancetty argent a chief indented azure (Sawbridge), 2nd and 3rd, Or
semy of trefoils slipped three crescents gules (Sawbridge of Wilts)
In pretence, and impaling, Sable a cross tau surmounted by a
crescent or (Wanley)
Motto: Post funera virtus
For Elizabeth, dau. of George Wanley, of London, who m. John
Sawbridge, of Olantigh, and d. 1733.   (B.L.G. 2nd ed.; O.H.S.)

2. All black background
Qly, as 1.   In pretence: Gules a plain long cross surmounting a
crescent inverted or (Wanley)
Crest: A demi-lion rampant azure, langued and armed gules, holding in
his paws a saw erect or   Mantling: Gules and argent
For John Sawbridge, who d. 20 Apr. 1762.   (Sources, as 1.)

3. Sinister background black
Sawbridge, impaling, Sable ten roundels, four, three, two and one
argent, on a chief argent a lion passant sable ermined argent langued
gules (Bridgeman)
Motto: In coelo quies   Two cherubs' heads above shield
For Mary Diana, dau. of Sir Orlando Bridgman, 4th Bt., who m. 1763,
as his 1st wife, John Sawbridge, of Olantigh, and d. 28 Jan. 1764.
(Sources, as 1.)

4. All black background
On a lozenge surmounted by a cherub's head
Sawbridge   In pretence: Gules on a bend or ermined sable three
leopards' faces azure langued gules (Stephenson)
Motto: Spes mea est in Agno
For Anne, dau. of Sir William Stephenson, who m. 1766, as his 2nd
wife, John Sawbridge, of Olantigh, and d.   (Sources, as 1.)

5. All black background
Sawbridge, impaling, Ermine a lion passant guardant gules armed and
langued azure (Ellis)
Crest and mantling: As 2.   Motto: Resurgam
For Samuel Elias Sawbridge, of Olantigh, who m. 1784, Elizabeth, dau.
of Brabazon Ellis, of Wyddiall Hall, Herts, and d. 27 May, 1850.
(Sources, as 1.; M.I.)

6. Sinister background black
Qly of six, 1st, Chequy or and azure on a chief gules three ostrich
feathers in plume or (Drax), 2nd, Gules three escallops within a bordure
engrailed argent (Erle), 3rd, Sawbridge, 4th, Sawbridge of Wilts, 5th,
Wanley, as 1, 6th, Stephenson   In pretence: Qly, 1st, Drax, 2nd and
3rd, Erle, 4th, Sable a garb or (Grosvenor)
Motto: Mort en droit   Cherub's head above and one at each side of shield
For Jane Frances, heiress of Richard Erle-Drax-Grosvenor, who m.
1827, John Samuel Wanley Sawbridge, of Olantigh, and d. 25 Dec.
1853.   (Sources, as 1.)

7. All black background
Arms: As 6.
Crests: Dexter, A demi-dragon wings endorsed or   Centre, A lion's
head erased or pierced in the neck with a spear proper   Sinister,
A demi-lion rampant azure holding in his paws a saw erect or
Mantling: Gules and argent   Motto: Mort en droit
For John Samuel Wanley Sawbridge-Erle-Drax (assumed the additional
names of Erle-Drax on his marriage) who d. 5 Jan. 1887.
(Sources, as 1.)

8. Dexter background black
Gules two arrows in saltire points downwards argent between three
buckles or over all a fess chequy argent and azure (Macaulay), impaling,
Sawbridge
Crest: A boot, couped above the ankle, sable, thereon a spur or
Mantling: Gules and argent   Mottoes: (above crest) Dulce periculum
(below shield) In coelo quies
For George Macaulay, M.D., who m. Catherine, dau. of John
Sawbridge, of Olantigh, and d. 1766.   (Sources, as 1.)

SURREY

by

Peach Froggatt

Mickleham 1: For Sir Lucas Pepys, 1st Bt., 1830
(Photograph by Mrs. M.R. Froggatt)

INTRODUCTION

In his general introduction Peter Summers points out that many hatchments have been destroyed during periods of restoration to English churches. A famous historian once said that 'restoration' when applied to churches should be expunged from the English dictionary and replaced by 'destruction'. We learn from old engravings, paintings and records that we have lost many hatchments. Kingston church contained 18 before restoration by a famous architect; there is now only one to be seen and we believe that this would have been lost had it not been in an inaccessible position. Our local church in Dorking contained seven, four of them Howard hatchments, the 11th and 12th Dukes of Norfolk being buried here. During the rebuilding of the new church in the mid-19th century they disappeared; the last one to be sighted many years ago was outside a junk shop. On the other hand Petersham lost many because years ago the P.C.C. made a rule that hatchments would only be allowed into the church for a limited period.

We have personally checked all the remaining hatchments and also discovered four in the bell tower of Betchworth church. Such was the condition of these that when photographed the person holding the hatchment could clearly be seen through the canvas. These have now been restored and replaced in the church. At Albury old church four were missing; one of these, for the Duke of Northumberland, had been removed to the new church and after many enquiries the hatchment of his wife Louisa was found in a serving room at Syon House, the London residence of the Duke of Northumberland. His Grace readily agreed to have it returned to Albury and now, fully restored, it has been reunited with its partner.

We are very lucky in Surrey in having many hatchments of famous people. At Kew there is a fine collection of royal funeral hatchments, not to be confused with the Royal Arms that appear in many churches; they include the hatchments of King George III and Queen Charlotte, King George IV, King William IV, the Duke and Duchess of Cumberland and the Duke of Cambridge, some of them being small hatchments that we believe were used to hang on the pulpit. The hatchment at Kingston Vale for H.R.H. Princess Mary, Duchess of Gloucester, d. 1857, is rectangular: it is painted on silk and was probably used to lay on the pall. Merton church has the hatchments of Horatio, Viscount Nelson and Sir William Hamilton. Both hatchments I believe we owe to the beautiful Emma. There is also the hatchment of Rear-Admiral Isaac Smith who served for a time under Capt. Cook, the circumnavigator, and is reputed to be the first European to set foot upon Australian soil. The oldest hatchment is in the chapel of Abbot's Hospital, Guildford, and is for George Abbot, Archbishop of Canterbury, who died in 1633. George Abbot was one of the six sons of Maurice and Alice Abbot, a clothworker and his wife, who lived in a cottage near the bridge at the foot of Guildford High Street. George was Archbishop of Canterbury for 22 years; he built the Hospital of the Blessed Trinity in Guildford in 1619, and helped to found Pembroke College, Oxford.

The hatchments for Hall at Walton-on-the-Hill showed no connection with monuments or records of the church although much was written about them living in the area, but the problem was solved by chance on a visit to Sutton parish church where a large monument for Ambrose Hall is to be seen outside the west door. It transpired that the son of Ambrose Hall had been vicar at Sutton at the time and had his parents buried there. A similar tale applies to Elizabeth Simon whose hatchment is in Merton church, but those tomb was traced to Wimbledon.

Information in church booklets regarding hatchments can be very misleading, and I have found a number of instances in the county where hatchments have been wrongly attributed.

I would like to take this opportunity to pay tribute to the work done by Mr. H. W. Pointer on the original survey

in 1952, by Mr. Anthony Pincott in the 1970s, and to thank
my husband Joss for escorting me on our many journeys
through Surrey and supplying the power for the back of our
tandem tricycle.

Peach Froggatt,
11, Rothes Road, Dorking

ALBURY, St Peter & St Paul

1. Sinister background black
Two shields   Dexter, within the Garter, Qly, 1st and 4th, qly i. & iv.
Or a lion rampant azure (Percy modern), ii. & iii. Gules three lucies
hauriant argent (Lucy), 2nd and 3rd, Azure five fusils conjoined in fess
or (Percy ancient)   Sinister, within a wreath, as dexter, with in
pretence, Qly, 1st and 4th, Or three bars wavy gules, 2nd and 3rd, Or a
lion's head erased within a tressure flory counterflory gules
(Drummond)
Duchess's coronet   Supporters: Dexter, A lion rampant azure
langued gules   Sinister, A lion rampant guardant, ducally crowned
or, gorged with a plain collar compony countercompony argent
and azure
For Louisa, dau. and co-heir of Henry Drummond, who m. 1845,
Algernon George, 6th Duke of Northumberland, K.G., and d. 18 Dec.
1890.   (B.P. 1963 ed.)

2. All black background
Within the Garter, Qly as dexter of 1.
Duke's coronet   Crest: On a chapeau gules and ermine a lion statant
tail extended azure   Motto: Esperance en Dieu   Supporters:
As 1, but sinister supporter collared compony argent and azure
For Algernon George, 6th Duke of Northumberland, K.G., who d. 2
Jan. 1899.   (B.P. 1963 ed.)

ASH

1. All black background
Qly, 1st and 4th, Vairy or and gules, on a chief engrailed azure a cross
crosslet between two lions rampant or (Hammersley), 2nd and 3rd,
Per bend indented sable and or ermined sable a bend between two
molets counterchanged (Spode)
Crests: Dexter, A lion rampant argent resting his sinister paw on a
dexter wing elevated or   Sinister, A demi-griffin wings elevated
gules between the claws a shield bearing the arms of Spode
Mantling: Gules and argent   Motto: Resurgam
For William Hammersley, of Ash Lodge, and co. Staffs, born William
Spode in 1776, but changed his name to Hammersley, c. 1831, and d.
27 May 1834, aged 58.   (M.I.)

BERMONDSEY

1. Dexter background black
Gules a lion passant argent entwined with a serpent proper, on a chief
embattled argent a sword erect between two laurel branches fructed
proper in bend sinister and in bend respectively (Gaitskell)   In
pretence: Sable a cinquefoil within a bordure engrailed ermine (Astley)
Crest: On a mountain an eagle reguardant wings expanded proper
collared azure resting the dexter claw on a roundel sable   Mantling:
Gules and argent   Motto: Fortitudo et integritas
For Thomas Gaitskell, J.P., D.L., who m. Joan Astley, and d. 14
Sept. 1839.   (M.I.)

2. Sinister background black
Gaitskell, in dexter chief a molet gules for difference, impaling, Gules
on a chevron or between three lions rampant argent three cinquefoils
sable (   )
Motto: Mors janua vitæ   Cherub's head on either side of shield
Possibly for Elizabeth, 1st wife of Henry Gaitskell, d. 26 July 1822,
aged 52.   (M.I.)

3. Dexter two-thirds background black
Gaitskell, as 2, impaling to the dexter, as 2, and to the sinister,
Qly, 1st and 4th, Or a lion rampant reguardant sable langued gules
(   ), 2nd and 3rd, Gules a chevron between three lions rampant
argent (   )
Crest, mantling and motto: As 1.
Possibly for Henry Gaitskell, who d. 4 Mar. 1836, aged 68.
(M.I.)

4. Dexter background black
Or a fess between three crosses formy fitchy sable (Riley), impaling,
Vert three buglehorns argent stringed or mouthpieces to dexter (   )
Crest: A dragon's head erased sable   Mantling: Gules and argent
Motto: Resurgam
Unidentified

5. Dexter background black
Qly, 1st and 4th, Gules on a fess argent three crosses formy sable, on a
canton or a spearhead or point argent (Newsom), 2nd and 3rd, Vert
three buglehorns stringed or (   ), impaling, Argent two bars and on
a chief azure three leopards faces or (Wright)
Crest: A sword erect proper   Mantling: Gules and argent   Motto:
Resurgam
Unidentified
(Now missing, probably destroyed in the fire in the gallery)

BETCHWORTH

1. All black background
On a lozenge surmounted by a countess's coronet
Qly, 1st and 4th, Argent a man's heart gules ensigned with an imperial
crown proper, on a chief azure three molets argent (Douglas), 2nd and
3rd, Argent three piles issuing from the chief gules, the exteriors
charged with a molet argent (Douglas of Dalkeith), impaling, Qly, 1st
and 4th, Ermine three roundels vert each charged with a cross or
(Heathcote), 2nd and 3rd, Azure a saltire engrailed ermine (Reyner)
Supporters: Two savages wreathed about their heads and waists with
oak leaves, each holding a club in his exterior hand, the great end on
the ground all proper   All within a mantle gules and argent
For Bridget, daughter of Sir John Heathcote, Bt., who m. as his 2nd
wife, James, 14th Earl of Morton, and d. at Betchworth, 2 Mar. 1805.
(B.P. 1963 ed.)

2. Dexter background black
Qly, 1st and 4th, Gules a bend engrailed or, in chief a molet and in base
a stag's head cabossed argent (Stable), 2nd and 3rd, Argent on a
chevron between three choughs sable three stags' heads cabossed argent
(   ), impaling, Azure two swords in saltire points upwards argent
pommelled and hilted or, in chief a molet or (   )
Crest: A castle argent thereon the cross of St George   Mantling:
Gules and argent   Motto: Resurgam
For John Stable, who m. Dorothy, and d. 22 Jan. 1795, aged 54.
(M.I.)

3. All black background
On a lozenge surmounted by a cherub's head
Arms: As 2, but field of impalement vert and molet argent
Motto: Resurgam
For Dorothy, widow of John Stable, d. 26 July 1832, aged 78.
(M.I.)

4. All black background
Qly, as dexter of 2.
Crest: As 2.   Mantling: Gules and argent   Motto: Resurgam
For John Edward, son of John and Dorothy, d. 29 Mar. 1796, aged 15.
(M.I.)
(These hatchments have all been restored by Lt.-Col. R. L. V.
ffrench-Blake)

LITTLE BOOKHAM

1. Dexter background black
Azure on a bend cotised between six lozenges or each charged with an

escallop sable five escallops sable (Pollen), impaling, Per pale azure and
gules two lions passant in pale or (Maddox)
Crest: A pelican in her piety per pale or and azure, on the wing a
lozenge or charged with an escallop sable, her young or   Mantling:
Gules and argent   Motto: Resurgam
For Edward Pollen, who m. Mary, dau. and co-heiress of Sir Benjamin
Maddox, 1st Bt., of Wormley, and d. 1731
(B.E.B.; Fortescue, People and Places)

2. All black background
On a lozenge surmounted by a cherub's head
Pollen (bend not cotised), impaling, Per pale gules and azure two lions
passant in pale or (Maddox)
Motto: Resurgam   Skull below
For Mary, widow of Edward Pollen, d. 26 June, 1744, aged 84.
(Source, as 1.; P.R.)

3. Dexter background black
Qly, 1st and 4th, Pollen with escallops on bend azure, 2nd and 3rd,
Azure a castle and in base a crescent or (Boileau), impaling, Azure a
chevron argent between three cranes' heads erased or langued gules (Hall)
Crests: Dexter, as 1, with lozenge argent   Sinister, A pelican in her
piety proper on the breast a saltire gules   Mantling: Gules and
argent   Motto: De tour mon coeur
For the Rev. George Pollen Boileau-Pollen, Rector of Little Bookham,
who m. 1824, Elizabeth, dau. of Sir James Hall, Bt., of Dunglass, and d.
7 Nov. 1847. She d. 26 Feb. 1873.
(B.L.G. 7th ed.; B.P. 1949 ed.)

4. All black background
On a lozenge surmounted by a cherub's head
Sable a fess ermine in chief three griffins' heads erased or langued gules
(Manningham)   In pretence: Pollen, with all escallops azure
Motto: Resurgam
For Anna Maria, dau. of the Rev. George Pollen, Rector of Little
Bookham, who m. Major General Coote Manningham, and d. 26 Aug.
1809.   (B.L.G. 7th ed.)

5. All black background
Qly, 1st and 4th, Argent a lion rampant sable armed and langued gules,
2nd and 3rd, Gules a chevron argent (Girardot), impaling, Argent on
a fess double cotised gules three griffins' heads erased or langued gules
(Dashwood)
Crest: A demi-lion rampant sable armed and langued gules   Mantling:
Gules and argent   Motto: Resurgam
For John Charles Girardot, of Allestree, Derbyshire, who m. Lydia

Marianne, dau. of Charles Vere Dashwood, of Stanford, Notts, and
d. 24 June 1845, aged 74. She d. 1 Oct. 1836, aged 66.
(B.P. 1949 ed.; church guide)

BRAMLEY

1. Dexter background black
Azure an eagle displayed argent armed or (Sparkes), impaling, Or a
cross gules charged with, in centre point a martlet or, at dexter and
sinister with a squirrel sejant argent, in chief with a lion passant argent
and in base with an annulet or (Page)
Crest: An eagle volant argent langued gules   Mantling: Gules and
argent   Motto: Resurgam   Winged skull below
For Richard Sparkes, who m. Frances (Page) and d. 14 June 1838,
aged 82. She d. 16 Feb. 1841, aged 76.   (M.I.)

BURSTOW

1. Dexter background black
Qly, 1st and 4th, Argent a chevron between three bulls passant
guardant gules, armed, unguled, membered and tails tufted or, each
crowned with an ancient crown or (Cole), 2nd and 3rd, Gules a lion
rampant argent between three pears or (Perry)   In pretence: Azure
a fess ermine flory counterflory or (Wallis)
For Edward Harold Cole, who m. Blanche Ruby Lavinia, dau. and
co-heir of Henry John Wallis, of Dulwich, and d. at Holly House,
Burstow, 1 Feb. 1963.
(Although this hatchment is no longer in Surrey it is included because
it was displayed in traditional manner at Holly House, the home of
his son, the present Garter Principal King of Arms, Sir Colin Cole)

CHELSHAM

1. All black background
Qly, 1st and 4th, Argent a chevron between three billets gules (Kelly),
2nd and 3rd, Argent a chevron between three talbots passant sable
(Talbot)
Crest: From a ducal coronet gules an ostrich's head and breast argent,
in the beak a horseshoe or   Mantling: Gules and argent   Motto:
In Deo fide nil desperandum
Probably for Alderman Thomas Kelly, Lord Mayor of London, 1836,
bur. 14 Sept. 1855, aged 83.   (P.R.)

CHIDDINGFOLD

1. Dexter background black
Sable ermined argent, on a cross quarter-pierced argent four millrinds
sable (Turnour), impaling, Argent on a pale azure three bulls' heads
couped or (Heys)
Earl's coronet   Crest: A lion passant guardant argent holding in
the forepaw a millrind sable   Motto: Esse quam videri
Supporters: Two lions argent semy of millrinds sable   All on a
mantle gules and ermine
For Edward, 3rd Earl Winterton, who m. 1809, Lucy Louisa, dau. of
John Heys, of Upper Sunbury, and d. 6 Jan. 1833.   (B.P. 1949 ed.)

2. All black background
On a lozenge   Arms: As 1.
Countess's coronet   Supporters: As 1.
For Lucy Louisa, widow of Edward, 3rd Earl Winterton, d. 26 Oct.
1846.   (B.P. 1949 ed.)

CHOBHAM

1. Sinister background black
Argent a chevron sable between three thorn trees proper (Thornton),
impaling, Vert a chevron between three millsails or (Milnes)
Motto: Resurgam   Shield suspended by bow of ribbon and festoon,
and with a cherub's head at each top corner
For Elizabeth, dau. of Robert Milnes, of Wakefield, who m. 1780,
Samuel Thornton, and d. 20 Mar. 1834. He d. 3 July 1838.
(B.L.G. 1937 ed.)

EAST CLANDON

1. Sinister background black
Sable ermined argent two chevrons or on the upper a crescent gules for
difference (Sumner), impaling, Argent a stag trippant proper (Holme)
Motto: In coelo quies   Shield suspended from festoons and a bow
of ribbon with a cherub's head at each top corner and a skull below
For Catherine, dau. of John Holme, of Holmé Hill, Cumberland, who
m. as his 1st wife, William Brightwell Sumner, and d. 30 Dec. 1777,
aged 41.   (B.L.G. 7th ed.)

2. Dexter background black
Sumner arms only   To dexter of main shield, Sumner impaling
Holme S.Bl.   To sinister of main shield, Sumner impaling, Argent

on a mount vert a tree proper over all on a fess azure three stars argent (Watson) D.Bl.
Crest: A lion's head erased argent langued gules ducally gorged or
Motto: In coelo quies   Cherub's head on either side of main shield
For William Brightwell Sumner, who was bur. 27 June 1796.   (P.R.)

3. Sinister background black
Qly, 1st and 4th, Sumner, 2nd and 3rd, Holme   In pretence:
Argent on a chevron sable three fishes hauriant argent (Pemble)
Motto: Resurgam   Two cherubs' heads above shield
For Louisa, dau. of Charles Pemble, who m. 1787, George Holme Sumner, of Hatchlands, and d. 14 Apr. 1816.
(B.L.G. 7th ed.; B. and B.)

4. All black background
Arms: As 3.
Crests: Dexter, as 2.   Sinister, A dove rising argent   Motto: Resurgam   Skull below
For George Holme Sumner, of Hatchlands, who m. 1787, Louisa, dau. of Charles Pemble, and d. 9 June 1838.
(B.L.G. 7th ed.; B. and B.)

5. Dexter background black
Qly, 1st and 4th, Sumner, 2nd and 3rd, Holme, impaling, Qly, 1st and 4th, Per pale gules and azure a wolf rampant or (Hankey), 2nd and 3rd, Argent a bear salient sable muzzled or (Barnard)
Crests: As 4.   Motto: Resurgam
For William Holme Sumner, who m. Mary Barnard, dau. of John Barnard Hankey, and d. 10 Sept. 1859.
(B.L.G. 7th ed.; B. and B.)

6. Sinister background black
Qly, 1st and 4th, Argent a cross engrailed between 12 billets gules (Heath), 2nd and 3rd, Qly argent and sable on a bend gules three lions passant or (Hubbart), impaling, Qly, 1st and 4th, Argent on a cross gules a royal crown proper (Augmentation), 2nd and 3rd, Argent a fess sable between three ravens proper (Nicholas)
Motto: Mors janua vitæ   Cherub's head above shield
For Bridget Nicholas, who m. Richard Heath, and d. 6 July 1745.
He d. 13 Feb. 1751.   (P.R.)

CLANDON Park

1. All black background
Qly, 1st and 4th, qly i. & iv. Argent a fess gules between six Cornish choughs proper (Onslow), ii. & iii. Argent on a bend azure three

martlets or (Harding), 2nd and 3rd, Argent on a cross sable a leopard's
face or (Bridges), impaling, Azure a chevron embattled counterembattled or (Hale)
Earl's coronet   Crest: An eagle sable preying on a partridge or
Motto: Festina lente   Supporters: Two falcons close proper
belled or
For Thomas, 2nd Earl of Onslow, who m. 2nd, Charlotte Hale, and
d. 22 Feb. 1827.   (B.P. 1963 ed.)

2. All black background
On a lozenge surmounted by a blue bow, and cherub's head below
Argent a fess gules between six Cornish choughs proper (Onslow)
Probably for Georgiana Charlotte Onslow, d. unm. 1829, or Elizabeth
Harriet Onslow, d. unm. 1837.   (B.P. 1963 ed.)

3. All black background
On a lozenge surmounted by a cherub's head and surrounded by a
golden tasselled cord arranged in four Stafford knots
Argent a fess gules between six Cornish choughs proper (Onslow)
Probably for Georgiana Charlotte Onslow, d. unm. 1829, or Elizabeth
Harriet Onslow, d. unm. 1837.   (Source, as 2.)

EGHAM

1. Sinister background black
Qly, 1st and 4th, Sable a cross patonce within a bordure or charged
with eight roundels sable (Ward), 2nd, Bendy of eight gules and or,
on a chief ermine two crosses formy gules (Hawkes), 3rd, Ermine on a
chevron vert between three buglehorns, mouthpieces to the dexter
sable stringed gules, an escallop or (Foster)   In pretence: Argent on
a bend gules between three roundels two and one sable three swans
argent (Clark)
Mantling: Gules and argent   Motto: Resurgam   Cherub's head above
For Ann, dau. and heir of Thomas Clark, of Greenham, Berkshire,
who m. 1815, Thomas Rawdon Ward, and d. 13 Aug. 1845.
(B.L.G. 7th ed.)

2. All black background
Arms: As 1.
Crest: A wolf's head erased proper langued gules gorged with a collar
sable charged with an escallop or between two bezants   Mantling:
Gules and argent   Motto: Garde la croix
For Thomas Rawdon Ward, d. 25 Feb. 1863.   (B.L.G. 7th ed.)
(Restored by Lt.-Col. R. L. V. ffrench-Blake in 1980)

ESHER, St George

1. Dexter background black
Sable a chevron ermine between three towers or (Spicer), impaling,
Gules a chevron between three dexter hands couped argent (Burn)
Crest: From a viscount's coronet proper an arm erect vested sable
cuffed argent the hand holding a fireball proper   Mantling: Gules
and argent   Motto: Resurgam
For John William Spicer, of Esher Place, who m. Mary Burn, and d.
1 Apr. 1831, aged 72.   (B.L.G. 1937 ed.; M.I. Christ Church)

2. All black background
On a lozenge surmounted by a cherub's head
Arms: As 1.
Motto: Resurgam
For Mary, widow of John Spicer, d. 7 Mar. 1835, aged 66.
(Sources, as 1.)

3. Dexter background black
Spicer, impaling, Qly, 1st and 4th, Gules a cross between four falcons
or (Webb), 2nd and 3rd, qly i. & iv. Argent on a bend between two
unicorns' heads erased azure three lozenges or (Smith), ii. & iii. Argent
on a chevron between three bells gules two bars gemel argent (Bell)
Crest and mantling: As 1.   Motto: Fortissimus qui se
For John William Gooch Spicer, who m. 1845, Juliana Hannah Webb,
dau. of the Rev. Edmund Probyn and Juliana Webb, and d. 1883.
(B.L.G. 1937 ed.)

4. All black background
Per chevron argent and gules a crescent counterchanged, on a chief
gules a unicorn's head couped between two leopards' faces or
(Chapman), impaling, Sable three molets argent (   )
Crest: A dove argent beaked and legged gules resting the dexter claw
on the band of a garb or   Mantling: Gules and argent
Motto: Resurgam
Probably for Thomas Chapman, d.   (M.I.)

FARNHAM

1. Sinister background black
Qly, 1st and 4th, Argent a stag's head cabossed gules attired or, on a
chief azure a cross crosslet fitchy or between two molets of six points
argent (Thomson), 2nd, Sable three swords in pile points downwards
argent pommels and hilts or, in dexter chief a crescent or for difference
(Poulett), 3rd, Argent a fret between four crescents sable (Buncombe),
impaling, Or on a canton sable a griffin's head erased or langued
gules (Jacob)

Cherub's head above and skull below
For Charlotte Jacob, who m. 1781, John Buncombe Poulett Thomson,
and d. in Paris, 18 May 1824.   (B.L.G. 1852 ed.; B. and B.)

2. All black background
On a lozenge surmounted by a skull   Or on a chevron sable three
lions rampant or (Lee), impaling, Argent on a fess sable between
six fleurs-de-lys gules two lions' paws erased in saltire ensigned with a
ducal coronet or (Andellaby)
Frame decorated with skulls and crossbones
For Susan, widow of Alexander (Lee), d. 1737.   (M.I.)

3. Dexter background black
Gules a boar's head couped argent between three Eastern crowns or
(Grant), impaling, Grant
Crest: On a mount vert a tree proper   Mantling: Gules and argent
Motto: Suo se robore firmat
For Charles Grant, who m. Charlotte, only dau. of John Grant, of
Bush Hill, Middlesex, and d. 23 Apr. 1823.   (B.L.G. 1937 ed.)

4. All black background
Within the Order of the Bath, Argent on a chevron engrailed gules
between three cross crosslets fitchy azure an Eastern crown between
two lions passant or, in centre chief the Badge of Ulster (Barlow)
Crest: From an Eastern crown or a demi-lion rampant argent holding
in the forepaws a cross crosslet fitchy azure   Mantling: Gules and
argent   Motto: Sis pius in primis   Supporters: Two angels
proper vested argent on the head an Eastern crown or the dexter
holding in the exterior hand a balance or and in the other a book
proper, the sinister bearing in the exterior hand an olive branch and in
the other a scroll proper
For Sir George Hilaro Barlow, 1st Bt., G.C.B., who m. 1789,
Elizabeth, dau. of Burton Smith, of Westmeath, and d. 18 Dec. 1846.
(B.P. 1949 ed.)

5. Sinister background black
Ermine a millrind sable (Mill), impaling, Argent three lozenges
conjoined in fess sable (   )   Motto: In morte quies
For Sophia, wife of Thomas Beddus Mill, bur. 3 Feb. 1806.
(P.R.)

6. All black background
On a lozenge surmounted by a skull
Mill, impaling, Ermine on a cross quarter pierced sable four millrinds
or (Turner)
Motto: In coelo quies
For Ann Turner, who m. George Mill, and d. 6 Sept. 1740, aged 61.
He d. 1737.   (B.L.G. 7th ed.; M.I.)

7. Black background to sinister half of sinister shield only
Two oval shields   Dexter, within the Garter, Gules a sword in bend
sinister proper between two keys wards upwards the upper or the
lower argent (See of Winchester), impaling, Ermine two chevrons
gules (Sumner)   Sinister, Sumner, impaling, Sable on a cross
or five crosses sable (Maunoir)
A bishop's mitre stringed or above shield
For Jennie, dau. of Dr. J. P. Maunoir, of Geneva, who m. 1816, the
Rt. Rev. Charles Richard Sumner, Bishop of Winchester, and d. 3 Sept.
1849.   He d. 15 Aug. 1874.
(Life of Bishop Sumner; B.L.G. 7th ed.)

8. All black background
Gules a chevron engrailed ermine between three eaglets close argent
langued and armed azure (Child)
Crest: On a rock proper an eaglet close argent langued and armed gules
holding in the beak a snake proper and ducally gorged or
Mantling: Gules and argent   Motto: In coelo quies
For Thomas Child, bur. 19 May 1855, aged 66.   (P.R.)

9. All black background
Qly, 1st and 4th, Per bend azure and or three griffins' heads erased
counterchanged, on a chief argent a fleur-de-lys between two roses gules
barbed and seeded proper (Rycroft), 2nd and 3rd, Per pale or and
sable a chevron between three fleurs-de-lys counterchanged (Nelson),
over all the Badge of Ulster   To dexter of main shield, as main
shield, impaling, Per pale or and argent a cross crosslet fitchy between
four fleurs-de-lys sable (Read) S.Bl.   To sinister of main shield, as
main shield, impaling, Gules an escarbuncle or (Mandeville) D.Bl.
Crest: A griffin's head erased per bend or and azure langued gules
charged with two fleurs-de-lys counterchanged   Mantling: Gules
and argent   Motto: In coelo quies
For Sir Nelson Rycroft, 2nd Bt., who m. 1st, 1791, Charlotte (d. 1803),
dau. of Henry Read, of Crowood, Wilts, and 2nd, Margaret, dau. of
Robert Mandeville, and d. 1 Oct. 1827.   (B.P. 1949 ed.)

10. All black background
On a lozenge surmounted by a cherub's head
Qly, 1st and 4th, Rycroft with chief or, 2nd and 3rd, Nelson, over all
the Badge of Ulster, impaling, Gules a Catherine wheel argent
(Mandeville)
For Margaret, widow of Sir Nelson Rycroft, 2nd Bt., d. 30 Mar. 1837.
(B.P. 1949 ed.)

11. All black background
On a lozenge surmounted by a cherub's head
Qly, 1st and 4th, Azure the sun in splendour or (Lothian), 2nd and 3rd,

Gules on a chevron argent three molets gules (Kerr)
Cherub's head below
For Elizabeth, dau. of William Crump, of Farnham, who m. Charles
Beauchamp, 2nd son of William, 5th Marquess of Lothian, and d.
10 Nov. 1830.   (B.P. 1949 ed.)

GATTON

1. Sinister background black
Qly, 1st and 4th, Sable on a cross engrailed or five roundels sable a
bordure engrailed or (Greville), 2nd, Azure fretty or (Willoughby), 3rd,
Gules a fess between six cross crosslets or (Beauchamp), impaling, Qly,
1st and 4th, Argent on a bend sable three owls argent (Savile), 2nd,
Gules a cross formy or (Golkar), Argent a bend sable between in
sinister chief an eagle displayed sable and in dexter base a cross crosslet
fitchy gules (Ryshworth)
Countess's coronet   Supporters: Dexter, A swan wings inverted
argent langued ducally gorged gules and legged sable   Sinister, A
lion or langued gules collared and chained azure, the collar charged
with three crescents argent
For Sarah Elizabeth, dau. of John, 2nd Earl of Mexborough, who m.
1816, Henry Richard, 3rd Earl of Warwick, and d. 30 Jan. 1851.
(B.P. 1949 ed.)
(There is another hatchment for Lady Warwick in St Mary's, Warwick)

2. Dexter background black
Or two chevrons gules (Monson), impaling, Argent a knight in full armour
affronté proper belted gules, on the head three ostrich feathers gules,
in the dexter hand a battleaxe and in the sinister hand a sword point
downwards proper (Blacker)
Baron's coronet   Crest: A lion rampant or supporting a pillar argent
Motto: Prest pour mon pais   Supporters: Dexter, A lion or langued
gules gorged with a collar azure charged with three crescents or and
chained azure   Sinister, A griffin argent langued gules collared
and chained as dexter
For Frederick John, 5th Baron Monson, who m. 1832, Theodosia,
youngest dau. of Latham Blacker, of Newent, Gloucs, and d.s.p. 7 Oct.
1841.   (B.P. 1949 ed.)
(There is another hatchment for Lord Monson at S. Carlton, Lincs)

3. Dexter background black
Monson, impaling, Ermine three leopards' faces or, on a chief gules a
lion passant guardant or (Larken)
Baron's coronet   Crest: As 2.   Supporters: Dexter, as 2, but
lined azure   Sinister, A griffin argent plain collared and lined azure

Motto: Pret pour mon pays
For William John, 6th Baron Monson, who m. 1828, Eliza, dau. of
Edmund Larken, of Bedford Square, and d. 17 Dec. 1862.
(B.P. 1949 ed.)
(There is another hatchment for Lord Monson at S. Carlton, Lincs)

4. All black background
On a lozenge surmounted by the coronet of a baroness
Arms: As 3.
Supporters: As 3.
For Elizabeth, widow of William John, 6th Baron Monson, d. 22 Jan.
1863.   (B.P. 1949 ed.)
(There is another hatchment for Lady Monson at S. Carlton, Lincs)

GUILDFORD, St Nicholas

1. All black background
Qly, 1st and 4th, Azure a cross moline lozenge pierced or (Molyneux),
2nd and 3rd, Azure on a cross argent five martlets sable (More),
impaling, Qly, 1st, Argent fretty azure, on each intersection a bezant
or, on a canton gules a lion's head erased or langued azure (Lowndes),
2nd, Sable on a bend argent three escallops gules (Layton), 3rd, Argent
on a bend azure three wolves' heads erased argent (Lowe), 4th, Or two
lions passant in pale between three cross crosslets fitchy two and one
sable (Garth)
Crests: Dexter, From a chapeau gules and ermine a peacock's feather
proper   Sinister, From a ducal coronet or an antelope trippant
argent   Motto: Resurgam   Palm branches flank shield
In view of background perhaps used first for husband and later for
widow. James More-Molyneux, of Loseley Park, m. 1832, Caroline
Isabella, eldest dau. of William Francis Lowndes-Stone, of Brightwell
Park, Oxon, and d. 9 Apr. 1874. She d. 5 Sept. 1888.
(B.L.G. 1937 ed.)

Abbot's Hospital

1. Sinister background black
On a cartouche surmounted by a mitre tasselled or
Azure an archiepiscopal staff in pale argent ensigned with a cross
formy or surmounted by a pall argent edged and fringed or charged
with four crosses formy fitchy sable (See of Canterbury), impaling,
Gules a chevron between three pears pendent stalked or, a molet
sable on the chevron for difference (Abbot)

Cherub's head and palm branches in base
For George Abbot, Archbishop of Canterbury, founder of Abbot's
Hospital, who d. 4 Aug. 1633.   (M.I.)

HAM

1. Sinister background black
Two shields   Dexter, within Order of the Thistle, Qly, 1st and 4th,
Argent a fret sable (Tollemache), 2nd and 3rd, Azure an imperial
crown or between three molets argent and a double tressure flory
counterflory or (Murray)   Sinister, Qly, 1st and 4th, Gules three
clarions or (Granville), 2nd and 3rd, Gules four fusils conjoined in fess
argent (Carteret)
Countess's coronet   Motto: Confido conquiesco   Supporters:
Dexter, An antelope proper, attired, mane and tip of tail or
Sinister, A winged stag attired gules   Cherub's head below
For Grace, eldest dau. of John, 1st Earl Granville, who m. 1729,
Lionel, 3rd Earl of Dysart, K.T., and d. 23 July 1755.   (B.P. 1949 ed.)

2. All black background
Within Order of the Thistle, with Badge pendent below, Qly, 1st and
4th, Argent a fret sable, in sinister chief the Badge of Ulster
(Tollemache), 2nd and 3rd, Murray
Earl's coronet   Crest: A horse's head couped argent maned or
between two wings expanded or semy of roundels sable   Motto:·
Confido conquiesco   Supporters: Two antelopes proper attired
and unguled or
For Lionel, 3rd Earl of Dysart, who d. 10 Mar. 1770.   (B.P. 1949 ed.)

E. HORSLEY

1. Dexter background black
Gules a saltire couped and in chief a rose argent barbed vert (Currie),
impaling, Gules a fess between three cross crosslets fitchy or (Gore)
Crest: A cock gules   Mantling: Gules and argent   Motto: Semper
virtute vigilans   Half a skull in dexter base
For William Currie, of East Horsley Park, who m. 1795, Percy, dau. of
Francis Gore, and d. 3 June 1829.   (B.L.G. 5th ed.; M.I.)

KEW

1. All black background
Within the Garter, Qly, 1st and 4th, Gules three lions passant guardant

in pale or (England), 2nd, Or a lion rampant within a tressure flory
counterflory gules (Scotland), 3rd, Azure a harp or stringed argent
(Ireland)   Over all an escutcheon tierced per pale and per chevron,
1st, Gules two lions passant guardant or (Brunswick), 2nd, Or semy
of hearts gules a lion rampant azure (Luneburgh), 3rd, Gules a horse
courant argent (Hanover), on an escutcheon gules the crown of
Charlemagne proper, the whole surmounted by a crown
Crest: On a crown proper a lion statant guardant or royally crowned
proper   Motto: Dieu et mon droit   Supporters: Dexter, A lion
rampant guardant or royally crowned proper   Sinister, A unicorn
argent, horned, hoofed, maned and gorged with an open crown and
chain reflexed over the back or;   roses, thistles and shamrocks
arranged around the motto
For King George III, who m. 1795, Caroline, dau. of Charles, Duke of
Brunswick Wolfenbuttel, and d. 7 Aug. 1821.

2. Small pulpit hatchment, as 1. with GIIIR flanking crest

3. Sinister background black
Two oval shields   Dexter, within the Garter, Royal arms modern
with escutcheon of Hanover   Sinister, within wreath, Qly of six,
1st, Or a buffalo's head cabossed sable armed and ringed argent
crowned and langued gules (Mecklenberg), 2nd, Azure a griffin
segreant or (Principality of Wenden), 3rd, Per fess, in chief azure a
griffin segreant or and in base vert a bordure argent (Principality of
Schwerin), 4th, Gules a cross formy argent crowned or (Ratzeberg),
5th, Azure a dexter arm issuant from clouds in sinister and holding
a finger ring or, scarf tied at the elbow or (Count of Schwerin),
6th, Or a buffalo's head in profile sable armed argent crowned and
langued gules (Lordship of Rostock)   Over all an inescutcheon, Per
fess gules and or (Stargard)
Royal crown above   Supporters: Dexter, A lion guardant or
royally crowned   Sinister, A unicorn argent, horned, maned,
hoofed and gorged with an open crown and chain reflexed over the
back or
For Queen Charlotte, wife of King George III, d. 17 Nov. 1818.

4. Small pulpit hatchment, as 3, with the letters Q.C. above crown

5. Identical to 1.
For King George IV, d. 26 June 1830.

6. Small pulpit hatchment, as 5, with GIVR flanking crest

7. All black background
Two oval shields   Dexter, Within the ribbon of the Order of St
George, with motto, Nunquam Retronium, Royal arms modern, with

escutcheon of Hanover uncrowned, in chief a label of three points argent charged on the centre with a fleur-de-lys azure and on the outer with a cross gules   Sinister, within a laurel wreath, Qly of six, 1st, Mecklenburg, 2nd, Principality of Wenden, 3rd, Principality of Schwerin, 4th, Ratzeburg, 5th, County of Schwerin, 6th, Lordship of Rostock, over all an escutcheon, Stargard   Crown of Hanover above   Supporters: Dexter, A lion guardant or royally crowned and with a label as in the arms   Sinister, A unicorn argent, horned, hoofed, maned and gorged with an open crown and chain reflexed over the back or and with a label as in the arms

For Ernest Augustus, Duke of Cumberland, de jure, King of Hanover, who m. 1815, Frederica, dau. of Charles, Duke of Mecklenberg Strelitz, and d. 18 Nov. 1851.

8. Sinister background black
Small pulpit hatchment, as 7, with letters Q and H on either side of crown
For Frederica, Duchess of Cumberland, Queen of Hanover, d. 29 June 1841.

9. Dexter background black
Two oval shields   Dexter, within the Garter, Qly, 1st and 4th, England, 2nd, Scotland, 3rd, Ireland, over all the crowned escutcheon of Hanover   Sinister, within a wreath of oakleaves, Qly of 17, 1st, Azure a lion barry argent and gules armed langued and crowned or (Landgrave of Thuringia), 2nd, Gules an escarbuncle or over all an escutcheon argent (Cleves), 3rd, Or a lion rampant sable (Meissen), 4th, Or a lion rampant sable (Julich), 5th, Argent a lion rampant gules crowned azure (Berg), 6th, Azure an eagle displayed or (Palatinate of Saxony), 7th, Or two pallets azure (Landsberg), 8th, Sable an eagle displayed or (Palatinate of Thuringia), 9th, Or semy of hearts gules a lion passant sable crowned gules (Orlamunde), 10th, Argent three bars azure (Elsenberg), 11th, Azure a lion rampant per fess or and argent (Tonna in Gleichen), 12th, Argent a rose gules barbed and seeded or (Burgaviate of Altenburg), 13th, Gules plain (Sovereign Rights), 14th, Argent three beetles' pincers gules (Engern), 15th, Or a fess chequy gules and argent (Marck), 16th, Per pale, Gules a column argent crowned or (Roemhild), Or on a mount vert a cock sable wattled gules (Hennenberg), 17th, Argent three chevronels (Ravensberg)   Over all an inescutcheon barry of ten or and sable a crown of rue in bend vert (Saxony)
Royal crest, supporters and motto   Rose, thistle and shamrock arranged below
For King William IV, who m. 1818, Adelaide, dau. of George, Duke of Saxe-Meiningen, and d. 20 June 1837.

10. Small pulpit hatchment, as 9, with the letters W, IV and R flanking crest

11. Dexter background black

Two oval shields   Dexter, within the Garter, Qly, 1st and 4th,
England, 2nd, Scotland, 3rd, Ireland, over all the escutcheon of
Hanover uncrowned, in chief a label of three points argent charged
on the centre with a cross gules and on the outer with two hearts in
pale gules   Sinister, within a wreath of oak leaves, Qly of nine,
1st, hidden, 2nd, in chief qly i. & iv. Or three chevronels gules (Hanau),
ii. & iii. Barry gules and or (Risnee), over all an inescutcheon per fess
gules and or (Muentzenburg), and in base, Or a lion rampant gules
crowned gules (Katzenelbogen), 3rd, Argent a patriarchal cross gules
(Hersfeld), 4th, hidden, 5th, Per fess sable and or in chief two molets of
eight points argent (Nidda), 6th, hidden, 7th, Gules two lions passant
in pale or (Dietz), 8th, Argent two bars sable (Isenberg), 9th, Gules
an escutcheon per fess argent and gules (Schaumberg), over all an
inescutcheon, Azure a lion rampant barry argent and gules crowned or
(Hesse)
Royal coronet with lion statant or crowned with a royal coronet
Supporters: Dexter, A lion or crowned with a royal coronet and
charged on the shoulder with a label as in the arms   Sinister, A
unicorn argent, horned, hoofed, maned and gorged with an open crown
and chain reflexed over the back or, and charged on the shoulder with
a label as in the arms
For Adolphus, Duke of Cambridge, K.G., who m. 1818, Augusta,
dau. of the Landgrave Frederick of Hesse-Cassel, and d. 8 July 1850.

KINGSTON-UPON-THAMES

1. Dexter background black

Argent on a fess embattled counterembattled gules three fleurs-de-lys
or (Disney), impaling, Argent three trees couped proper (   )
Crest: A lion's head erased gules semy-de-lys or murally gorged argent
Mantling: Gules and argent   Motto: In coelo quies
Possibly for William Disney, d. 22 Apr. 1830, aged 70.   (M.I.)

KINGSTON VALE

1. All black background

An oval shield and lozenge   Dexter, shield, within the Garter, Qly,
1st and 4th, England, 2nd, Scotland, 3rd, Ireland, over all per pale
and per chevron, Brunswick, Luneberg and Westphalia, not surmounted
by crown and no crown of Charlemagne; a label of five points argent,
a fleur-de-lys azure on centre point and on each other a cross gules
Lozenge, Qly, 1st and 4th, England, 2nd, Scotland, 3rd, Ireland, a label

of three points argent, on the centre point a rose gules and on each of
the other a canton gules, over all, Brunswick, Luneberg and Westphalia,
uncrowned and no crown of Charlemagne   Above, a royal
princess's crown   On silk, not canvas
Rectangular, c. 24 in. x 18 in.
For Princess Mary, 4th dau. of King George III, who m. William
Frederick, 2nd Duke of Gloucester, K.G., and d. 30 Apr. 1857.

LEIGH

1. All black background
Per bend nebuly sable and or two bendlets between six escallops all
counterchanged (Freshfield), impaling, Ermine three increscents
gules (Sims)
Crest: The Angel Gabriel in armour proper vested argent charged with a
cross patonce gules on the breast, belted, winged and crined or, the
head surmounted by a cross patonce gules, holding in the hands a spear
or   Mantling: Sable and argent   Motto: Nobilitatis virtus non
stemma character
For Charles Kaye Freshfield, who m. Elizabeth Sims, and d. 1891.
She d. 1849.   (B.L.G. 1921 ed.)

2. All black background
Qly argent and azure on the 2nd and 3rd quarters a molet or ermined
sable over all on a bend invected plain cotised sable three cinquefoils
ermine, in centre chief a crescent gules for difference (Dendy)
Crest: A bezant charged with a unicorn's head couped azure between
two slips of lauristinus vert   Mantling: Gules and argent
Motto: Resurgam
Probably for Richard Caffyn Dendy, d. 22 Oct. 1832, aged 74.   (M.I.)

LINGFIELD

1. Sinister background black
Qly, 1st and 4th, Qly azure and gules three crescents one in centre two
in base argent between three saltires couped two and one or (Lane),
2nd, Or a bend vair cotised gules (Bowyer), 3rd, Gules a bezant
between three demi-lions rampant argent (Bennett), impaling,
Argent a chevron gules between three leopards' faces sable (Farindon)
Motto: Cede Deo   Shield suspended from bow of ribbon, with a
cherub's head at each upper angle
For Louisa, eldest dau. of James Farindon, who m. Thomas Lane, and
d. 2 May 1832, aged 51. He d. 26 Dec. 1859, aged 87.   (M.I.)

MERTON

1. Dexter background black

Within the Order of the Bath, Or a cross flory sable surmounted by a
bend gules thereon a bend engrailed or charged with three hand
grenades sable fired proper, a chief of Augmentation argent thereon
waves of the sea from which issuant in the centre a palm tree between
a disabled ship on the dexter, and a ruinous battery on the sinister
proper (Nelson)   Shield surmounted by a ducal coronet or, and
above it a viscount's coronet
Crests: Dexter, From a naval crown or the chelengk or diamond plume
of triumph, presented to Lord Nelson by the Grand Seignior
Sinister, The stern of the St Joseph, first rate man-of-war floating in
waves of the sea proper   Supporters: Dexter, A sailor habited
and armed with a cutlass and pair of pistols in his belt proper his right
hand supporting a pike proper thereon hoisted a commodore's flag
argent and his left holding a palm branch   Sinister, A lion
reguardant, in his mouth two broken flag staffs, flowing from the one
the Spanish and from the other the French tricoloured ensign, and in
the forepaw a palm branch all proper, each supporter standing on a
motto scroll, the dexter carrying the words, Palmam qui, the sinister
carrying the words, Ferat meruit   Pendent from behind and from
the dexter side of the ribbon of the Bath two pink ribbons bearing a
clasp with the date 1801   Pendent from behind and from the
sinister side by a ribbon vert the Star of the Order of St Joachim
Pendent from the centre base of the shield three ribbons azure
fimbriated gules three medals   Pendent from dexter and sinister
sides of the shield a ribbon azure fimbriated gules depending from
this the Order of St Ferdinand and of Merit and from this the Order
of the Crescent
For Horatio, Viscount Nelson, who d. 21 Oct. 1805.   (B.P. 1949 ed.)

2. Dexter background black

Within the Order of the Bath, on a mantle gules and ermine, Qly, 1st
and 4th, qly i. & iv. Gules three pierced cinquefoils ermine (Hamilton),
ii. & iii. Argent a lymphad sails furled sable (Arran), 2nd and 3rd,
Argent a heart gules ensigned with an imperial crown proper on a chief
azure three molets argent (Douglas)
Crest: From a ducal coronet or an oak tree vert fructed or and
penetrated transversely in the main stem by a frame saw proper
Mottoes: (above crest) Through   (below shield) Sola nobilitat
virtus   Supporters: Two antelopes argent each ducally gorged,
chained and unguled or, and charged on the shoulder with a molet or
For Sir William Hamilton, K.B., who d.s.p. 6 Apr. 1803.   (B.P. 1949 ed.)

3. Sinister background black

Argent a bugle horn stringed sable in chief three leaves vert (Burnett),

impaling, Argent on a bend azure three stags' heads cabossed argent
(Fassett)
Motto: In coelo quies   Shield hanging from ribbon tied with
festoons in a bow, at each upper corner a cherub's head
For Anne Fassett, who m. Sir Robert Burnett, Sheriff of London, and
d. 12 June 1802.   (B. and B.)

4. All black background
Per saltire gules and vert over all a sword erect in pale proper
interlaced with a bugle horn stringed or, on a chief embattled or
ermined sable three leaves vert (Burnett), impaling, Argent on a bend
azure three stags' heads cabossed argent (Fassett)
Crest: From a mural coronet or on a mount a vine vert fructed or; out
of clouds to the sinister a man's hand issuant grasping a knife in the
act of pruning proper   Mantling: Gules and argent   Motto: Resurgam
For Sir Robert Burnett, who d. 23 June 1816.   (Source, as 3.)

5. All black background
Sable ermined argent three bezants (Smith)
Crest: A demi-wildman proper holding in the dexter hand a bunch of
barley vert and wreathed round the temples with leaves proper
Mantling: Gules and argent   Motto: In coelo quies   In saltire
behind the shield a white and blue flag; below these a red flag and the
white ensign
For Rear-Admiral Sir Isaac Smith, d. 2 July 1831, aged 78.   (B. and B.)

6. All black background
On a lozenge surmounted by a cherub's head
Azure a chevron between three trefoils slipped argent (for Simon),
impaling, Gules three fleurs-de-lys argent (Masterman)
Motto: Resurgam
For Elizabeth, widow of Henry Simon, d. 21 Mar. 1798, aged 75.
(Manning and Bray)

MICKLEHAM

1. Dexter background black
Sable on a bend or between two horses' heads erased argent three
fleurs-de-lys sable, in centre chief the Badge of Ulster (Pepys)   In
pretence (surmounted by a countess's coronet): Qly, 1st and 4th,
Argent on a bend azure three oval buckles tongues upwards or (Leslie),
2nd and 3rd, Or a lion rampant gules debruised by a bend azure
(Abernethy); also impaling, Sable a fess or between three asses argent
(Askew)
Crest: A camel's head erased proper ducally gorged and lined or

Mantling: Gules and argent   Motto: Mens cujusque is est quisque
For Sir Lucas Pepys, 1st Bt., who m. 1st, 1772, Jane Elizabeth,
Countess of Rothes, who d. 2 June 1810; and 2nd, 1813, Deborah,
dau. of Anthony Askew, and d. 17 June 1830.   (B.P. 1949 ed.)

2. All black background
Pepys, in centre chief the Badge of Ulster, impaling, Sable on a fess
engrailed between six sprigs of oak fructed or three oak leaves vert, a
bordure ermine (Oakes)
Crest: A camel's head erased or ducally gorged, muzzled and lined
sable   Mantling: Gules and argent   Motto: Resurgam
For Rev. Sir Henry Leslie, 3rd Bt., who assumed the name of Leslie
instead of Pepys, Rector of Sheephall, Herts, m. 1816, Elizabeth Jane,
dau. of the Rev. James Oakes, and d.s.p. 9 Dec. 1849.   (B.P. 1949 ed.)

3. Dexter background black
Per pale or and sable a chevron between three snafflebits all
counterchanged (Milner), impaling, Qly, 1st and 4th, Argent two
greyhounds courant in pale sable, on a chief azure three estoiles or
(Moore), 2nd and 3rd, Sable two pallets or over all on a fess gules
three fleurs-de-lys or (Moore)
Crest: Between two wings or a horse's head couped argent maned and
bridled or and charged on the neck with a bezant   Mantling: Gules
and argent   Motto: Resurgam
For Col. Charles William Milner, who m. 1843, Mary Jane, dau. of
R. Moore of Hampton Court Palace, and d.s.p. 31 May 1847.
(B.P. 1949 ed.)

4. Dexter background black
Or two lions passant guardant sable, on a chief azure three covered cups
or (Worrell), impaling, Or an eagle displayed sable langued and
clawed gules (   )
Crest: A lion's gamb erased and erect proper holding a covered cup or
Mantling: Gules and argent   Mottoes: (above crest) Modeste
(below shield) Resurgam
For Jonathan Worrell, of Juniper Hall, Mickleham, d. 1814. (B. and B.)

5. All black background
On a lozenge surmounted by a cherub's head
Qly, 1st and 4th, Argent a chevron between three crosses formy gules
(Barclay), 2nd and 3rd, Per fess argent and sable a fess per fess counter
embattled between three falcons counterchanged (Thompson)   In
pretence: Qly, 1st and 4th, Sable a lion rampant or (Brockhurst), 2nd
and 3rd, Gules a chevron between three pheons or (Arnold)
Motto: Resurgam
For Rebecca, only child of Benjamin Brockhurst, who m. 1782, George
Barclay of Burford Lodge, Surrey, and was bur. 29 Jan. 1838, aged 74.
(B.L.G. 2nd ed.; P.R.)

6. Sinister background black
Azure a fess wavy argent in chief three estoiles or (Jenkinson), impaling,
Argent on a fess gules between three peacocks close vert a lion passant
or between two combs argent (Penn)
Two cherubs' heads above shield
For Mary, wife of David Jenkinson, of Juniper Hall, d. 16 Oct. 1785.
(Tomb in churchyard)

7. Dexter background black
Qly, 1st, Argent on a mount in base vert three gillyflowers proper
stalked and leaved vert, on a chief azure four molets in fess argent
(Sperling), 2nd, Sable three snafflebits argent (Milner), 3rd, Argent a
chevron azure between three foxes' heads erased proper (Foxall),
4th, Gules a chevron embattled argent between in chief two martlets
argent and in base a dexter hand in fess proper vested and cuffed argent
holding a dagger erect argent pommel and hilt or (Piper)   In
pretence: Qly, 1st and 4th, Gules a lion rampant per fess argent and or
(Grace), 2nd and 3rd, Chequy argent and azure on a fess argent three
saltires couped azure (Cheney)
Crest: A molet between two wings argent   Mantling: Gules and
argent   Motto: Resurgam
For Henry Piper Sperling, who m. 1791, Sarah Anne, dau. and
co-heiress of Henry Grace, of Tottenham, and d. 6 Jan. 1847.
(B.L.G. 5th ed.)

8. All black background
Per fess azure and or a pale and three falcons two and one with wings
addorsed and belled each holding in the beak a padlock all counter-
changed, in centre chief a label sable (Lock), impaling, Azure a chevron
or between three bezants, on a chief ermine three cinquefoils gules
(Jennings)
Crest: A falcon as in the arms   Mantling: Gules and argent
Motto: Resurgam
For William Lock, who m. Elizabeth Jennings, and d. 15 Dec. 1847,
aged 80. She d. 15 May 1846, aged 65.   (M.I.)

MORDEN

1. Sinister background black
Gules a cross engrailed argent (Ridge)   In pretence: Vert a chevron
between three pheons or (Holman)
Motto: Resurgam   Shield pendent from bow of blue ribbons with a
cherub's head at each top angle
For Elizabeth Holman, who m. George Ridge, of Morden Park, and
d. 18 Feb. 1824, aged 74.   (M.I.; P.R.)

2. All black background
Arms: As 1.
Crest: From a mural coronet argent two arms in armour embowed
proper garnished or holding a spear argent headed or therefrom flowing
to the dexter a pennon argent charged with a cross gules   Mantling:
Gules and argent   Motto: Resurgam
For George Ridge, who d. 16 Oct. 1824, aged 78.   (Source, as 1.)

3. Dexter background black
Qly, 1st and 4th, Ridge, 2nd and 3rd, Vert a chevron ermine between
three pheons argent (Holman), impaling, Gules an inescutcheon within
an orle of eight molets argent (Chamberlayne)
Crest, mantling and motto: As 2.
For George Cooper Ridge, who m. Eleanor Martha Chamberlain, and
d. 24 Mar. 1842, aged 73. She d. 1873.   (Source, as 1.)

4. Sinister background black
Sable on a bend cotised or a rose gules barbed and seeded proper
between two annulets sable (Conway), impaling, Argent in chief issuing
from dexter and sinister two hands proper cuffed azure holding between
them a garland from which issues a branch vert, in base on a mount
vert a fox passant sable holding in the mouth a sprig vert (Schrom)
Crest: A bust of a Moor in profile couped at the shoulders proper
wreathed round the temples or and sable   Motto: In coelo quies
Lower part of shield terminates in wings   Cherub's head below
For Sophia Schrom, who m. Thomas Conway, and d. 24 Jan. 1785.
(Source, as 1.)

5. Sinister background black
Argent in chief on a bend gules an esquire's helmet or, in centre chief a
molet gules for difference (Tritton), impaling, Argent three greyhounds
courant in pale sable, in chief a crescent gules for difference (Biscoe)
Motto: Resurgam   Shield hangs from bow of blue ribbons with a
cherub's head at each top corner
For Mary, dau. of Vincent Hilton Biscoe, of Hookwood, Surrey, who
m. the Rev. Robert Tritton, Rector of Morden, and d. 20 Oct. 1835.
He d. 27 Nov. 1877.   (Source, as 1.)

6. All black background
Sable a double-headed eagle within a bordure engrailed argent, in
centre chief a label argent for difference (Hoare), impaling, Or fretty
gules a canton ermine (Noel)
Crest: An eagle's head erased argent charged with an ermine spot
Mantling: Gules and argent   Motto: Resurgam
For William Henry Hoare, of Broomfield House, Battersea, who m.
1807, Louisa Elizabeth, dau. of Sir Gerard Noel Noel, 2nd Bt., and d.
18 Sept. 1819.   (B.L.G. 1937 ed.)

7. All black background
Qly, 1st and 4th, Hoare, no label, 2nd and 3rd, Sable a falcon close or
(Bolton), impaling, Vert a chevron between three pheons or (Malortie)
Crest: An eagle's head couped argent charged with an ermine spot
and langued gules   Mantling and motto: As 6.
For Henry Hoare, of Mitcham, who m. 1775, Lydia Henrietta, dau.
and co-heir of Isaac Malortie, of London, and d. 15 Mar. 1828.
(B.L.G. 1937 ed.)

8. Sinister background black
Qly, 1st and 4th, Sable a double-headed eagle argent charged on the
breast with an ermine spot within a bordure engrailed argent (Hoare),
2nd and 3rd, Bolton   In pretence: Azure three bucks trippant
argent (Greene)
Motto: In coelo quies   Two cherubs' heads above shield
For Angelina Frances, 4th dau. and co-heiress of James Greene, of
Turton Manor, Lancs, who m. 1810, George Matthew Hoare, of
Morden Lodge, and d. 25 Jan. 1846. .   (B.L.G. 1937 ed.)

9. All black background
Qly, 1st and 4th, Hoare, as 8, 2nd and 3rd, Bolton, in centre chief a
molet gules for difference   In pretence: Greene
Crest and mantling: As 6.   Motto: In ardua
For George Matthew Hoare, d. 28 July 1852.   (B.L.G. 1937 ed.)

10. Dexter background black
Qly, 1st and 4th, Hoare, as 8, 2nd, Bolton, but charged on the breast
with a molet gules, 3rd, Argent three bucks trippant sable (Greene),
impaling, Qly, 1st and 4th, Or on a pile gules between six fleurs-de-lys
azure three lions passant guardant or (Seymour Augmentation), 2nd
and 3rd, Gules two wings conjoined in lure or (Seymour)
Crest: As 6.   Mantling: Sable and argent   Motto: In ardua
For Henry James Hoare, of Morden, who m. 1846, Julia Seymour
Traherne, dau. of Henry John Hyde Seymour, of Wells, and d. 10 Feb.
1859.   (B.L.G. 1937 ed.)

11. All black background
On a lozenge surmounted by a cherub's head
Qly of six, 1st, Sable on a chevron argent between three staves raguly
argent fired at the top proper a fleur-de-lys gules between two choughs
respectant proper (Meyrick), 2nd, Vert three eagles displayed in fess
or (Wynn), 3rd, Argent three cocks gules (Sais), 4th, Argent a chevron
sable between three choughs holding in their beaks an ermine spot
(Lloyd), 5th, Sable a chevron between three owls argent (Broughton),
6th, Gules a chevron between three lions rampant or (Owen)
In pretence: Or two lions passant in pale sable langued gules in chief
two cross crosslets fitchy sable (Garth)

For Clara, eldest dau. and heiress of Richard Garth, of Morden, who m.
Owen Putland Meyrick, of Bodorgan, and d. 29 Nov. 1826.
(B.L.G. 5th ed.)

12. Dexter background black
Qly, 1st and 4th, Argent three cinquefoils and a chief azure (Stone),
2nd and 3rd, Argent fretty azure, the interlacings each charged with a
bezant, on a canton gules a leopard's head erased or (Lowndes)   In
pretence: Or two lions passant in pale sable langued gules between
three cross crosslets fitchy two and one sable (Garth)
Crests: Centre, A leopard's head erased or gorged with a chaplet vert
Dexter, From a ducal coronet or a griffin's head and neck argent
between two wings or   Sinister, A goat statant argent attired or
Mantling: Gules and argent   Motto: Mediocria firma
For William Lowndes-Stone, who m. 1775, his cousin, Elizabeth, dau.
and co-heir of Richard Garth, of Morden, and d. 16 May 1830, aged 80.
(B.L.G. 5th ed.)

13. Dexter background black
Ermine on a chevron engrailed sable three cinquefoils or (Hatfield),
impaling, Ermine on a canton gules a chevron argent (Middleton)
Crest: A dexter cubit arm vested sable cuffed ermine, the hand proper
holding a rod tipped with a cinquefoil or   Mantling: Gules and
argent   Motto: In caelo quies
For John Hatfield, who m. Ann Middleton, and d. 9 Dec. 1791, aged
75. She d. 12 July 1794.   (B.L.G. 1852 ed.)

MORTLAKE

1. All black background
Sable on a chevron or between three fleurs-de-lys argent three cronels
sable (Reeves), impaling, Argent a chevron azure between three hawks
proper (Hawkes)
Crest: A demi-greyhound argent ducally gorged a line reflexed over the
back or holding between the paws a sprig vert   Mantling: Gules
and argent   Motto: Rien sans Dieu
For Frederick Reeves, who m. Catherine Hawkes, and d. 1842.
(Note in church)

2. Dexter background black
Qly, 1st and 4th, Per pale argent and sable three chevronels between
three cinquefoils all counterchanged (Ommaney), 2nd and 3rd,
Argent on a bend sable three molets argent (   ), over all a crescent
gules for difference, impaling, Argent a chevron between three hawks
azure (Hawkes)

Crest: A cubit arm erect vested per pale argent and sable cuffed argent
the hand proper holding a battleaxe in bend sinister proper
Mantling: Gules and argent   Motto: Resurgam
For Sir Francis Molyneux Ommaney, who m. Georgiana Frances
Hawkes, and d. 7 Nov. 1840. She d. 19 Sept. 1854.   (M.I.)

3. Dexter background black

Two oval shields   Dexter, within the order of Hanover, Argent three
roses gules barbed proper (for Best)   Sinister, within an ornamental
wreath, as dexter, impaling, Argent on a mount vert a beehive beset
by bees proper (   )
Baron's coronet   Crest: A mount vert from which grow three roses
gules barbed, stalked and leaved vert   Motto (above crest):
Ungesucht   Motto: (below shield): Nulli cedo fide   Supporters:
Dexter, A horse argent wreathed about the neck vert   Sinister, A
husbandman vested proper wreathed at the temples vert in the sinister
hand a spade proper
For Baron George Best, K.C.H., who m. Ann (d. 21 Mar. 1836,
aged 77), and d. 12 Mar. 1823, aged 67.   (M.I.)

4. All black background

On a lozenge surmounted by a cherub's head
Qly, 1st and 4th, Azure a lion rampant argent langued gules debruised
by a bend gules charged with three escallops argent (Taylor), 2nd
Sable six lions rampant argent (   ), 3rd, Argent a chevron gules
between three trefoils slipped vert (   ), impaling, Gules three trees
eradicated proper (   )
Motto: Resurgam
For Mrs. Elizabeth Taylor, d. 8 May 1837, aged 72.   (M.I.)

PETERSHAM

1. All black background

Azure three bears' heads couped argent muzzled gules (Forbes),
impaling, two coats per fess, in chief, Argent a cross of lozenges azure
over all a bend compony ermine and azure (Braddyll); in base, Gules
three fleurs-de-lys or (   )
Crest: A hand, vested argent, fesswise holding a dagger erect pommel
and hilt or the point piercing a bear's head couped argent muzzled gules
Mantling: Azure and argent   Motto: Spes mea Deus
For Gordon, eldest son of General Gordon Forbes, who m. Margaret,
dau. of Wilson Gale Braddyll, and d.
(B.L.G. 2nd ed.)

SEALE

1. Dexter background black

Qly, 1st and 4th, Ermine on a chief sable a griffin passant argent (Chester), 2nd, qly i. & iv. Azure three eagles' legs couped or (Gambon), ii. & iii. Or a Moor's head in profile couped sable wreathed at the temples argent (   ), over all an escutcheon, Or a pomegranate slipped proper (Granado), 3rd, Or on a chevron between three cinquefoils azure three escallops argent, on a chief per pale gules and or a griffin passant argent (Hawkins), impaling, Chester with a crescent gules for difference
Crest: A griffin passant ermine langued gules   Mantling: Sable and argent   Motto: Vincit qui patitur
For Frederick James Chester, who m. 1847, his cousin, Charlotte Ellen, dau. of Charles Chester, and d. 24 May 1883.
(B.L.G. 1937 ed.)

2. All black background

Qly, 1st, Gules on a chevron argent three stags' heads erased sable a chief per fess nebuly sable and argent (Woodroffe), 2nd, Sable a fess ermine between two mountain cats passant guardant argent (Hill), 3rd, Per fess or and azure a pale counterchanged and three lions' heads erased gules langued or, on the azure three fountains argent and vert (White), 4th, Per chevron engrailed gules and argent three talbots' heads erased counterchanged (Duncombe)   To dexter of main shield, Woodroffe, impaling, Argent a fret sable a canton gules (Vernon) A.Bl.   To sinister of main shield, Woodroffe, impaling, Qly, 1st and 4th, Gules a chevron ermine between three eagles close argent (Childe), 2nd and 3rd, Qly per fess indented or ermined sable and azure (Lacon) A.Bl.
Crest: A dexter arm embowed habited with leaves vert, in the hand a branch of honeysuckle proper   Mantling: Gules and argent
Motto: In coelo quies   Cherub's head at each top angle of shield and winged skull in base
For George Woodroffe, son of Robert Woodroffe and Hester Duncombe, who m. 1st, Ann Vernon (d. 1769), and 2nd, Anne, dau. of William Lacon Childe, and d. 30 Nov. 1779. She d. May 1774.
(Manning and Bray)

3. All black background (should be sinister black)

Sable a lion passant argent in dexter paw a cross crosslet fitchy or, on a chief argent three cross crosslets sable (Long), impaling, Or on a fess between two chevrons sable three cross crosslets or (Walpole)
Motto: (above shield) In coelo quies
For Catherine, dau. of Horatio, 2nd Earl of Orford, who m. 1822, Henry Lawes Long, and d. suddenly from alarm in a thunderstorm, 20 Aug. 1867.   (B.L.G. 5th ed.; B.P. 1875 ed.)

4. All black background
Arms: As 3.
Crest: From a duke's coronet or a lion's head argent gutty gules,
langued gules   Two mottoes flanking crest: Dexter, Div. res.
Sinister, Si qua div   Motto: (below shield) Pieux quoique preux
For Henry Lawes Long, who d. 1868.   (Sources, as 3.)

SHALFORD

1. Dexter background black
Azure a chevron argent between three doves close or (Austen)   In
pretence: Or two bars and in chief a lion passant azure (Gregory)
Crest: A dove rising or standing on a leopard's head azure
Mantling: Gules and argent   Motto: Resurgam
For Robert Austen, who m. 1772, Frances Annesley, dau. and heir of
John Wentworth Gregory, and d. 3 Nov. 1797.   (B.L.G. 1937 ed.)

2. Sinister background black
Austen, impaling, Gules on a fess cotised between in chief two birds
each holding a sprig of leaves in its beak and in base a ducal coronet or
three molets sable (Bate)
Motto: Ne quid nimis   Shield pendent from a bow of ribbons and
with a cherub's head at each top corner
For Anne Amelia, only dau. of Robert Spearman Bate, who m. 1805,
as his 1st wife, Sir Henry Edmund Austen, of Shalford House, and d.
5 Sept. 1839.   (B.L.G. 1937 ed.)

3. All black background
Austen, impaling two coats per fess, in chief, Gules on a fess cotised
between in chief two birds and in base a ducal coronet or three
molets sable (Bate), and in base, Or on a bend sable three legs in armour
couped at the thigh and erased at the ankle or and argent, on a canton
sinister sable a saltire or (Blagrave)
Crest, mantling and motto: As 1.
For Sir Henry Edmund Austen, who m. 1st, Anne Amelia, only dau. of
Robert Spearman Bate, and 2nd, Catherine, widow of Sir Robert
Pocklington, and dau. of John Blagrave, of Calcot Park, Reading,
and d. 1871.   (B.L.G. 1937 ed.)

4. Dexter background black
Austen   In pretence: Gules two lions passant or on a canton or
three annulets gules (Godwin)
Crest: As 1.   Mantling: Azure and argent   Motto: Ne quid nimis
For Robert Alfred Cloyne Godwin-Austen, who m. Maria Elizabeth,
dau of Major-Gen. Sir Henry T. Godwin, K.C.B., and d. 25 Nov. 1884.
(B.L.G. 1937 ed.)

SOUTHWARK Cathedral

1. All black background
Gules a cross moline argent square pierced sable, on a chief or three
birds volant azure (? for Barchard)
Helm, but no crest   Mantling: Gules and argent   Motto: Resurgam
Skull below
Possibly for Joseph Barchard, who d. 1770.   (College of Arms)

2. Dexter background black
Argent two bars azure on a chief azure a fleece argent banded between
two millrinds erect or (Barchard), impaling, Gules semy of cross
crosslets fitchy argent a bend vairy or and azure (Howard)
Crest: A dove argent winged or in the bill an olive branch proper
collar and legs gules the dexter claw resting on a millrind erect azure
Mantling: Gules and argent   Motto: Morior ut vivam
For John Barchard, of Wandsworth, who m. 2nd, Elizabeth, dau. of
Matthew Howard, and d. Oct. 1816.   (College of Arms)

3. All black background
On a lozenge surmounted by a cherub's head
Arms: As 2.   Motto: As 2.
For Elizabeth, widow of John Barchard, d. Jan. 1827, aged 66.
(Source, as 2.)

TATSFIELD

1. Dexter background black
Qly, 1st and 4th, Barry of eight argent and gules over all a cross
patonce sable (Gower), 2nd and 3rd, Azure three leaves or (Leveson),
impaling, Argent three stags' heads erased proper a bordure counter-
compony or and azure (Doyle)
Crest: A wolf passant argent collared and lined or   Mantling: Gules
and argent   Motto: Frangas non flectes
For William Leveson-Gower, of Titsey Place, who m. 1834, Emily
Josephine Eliza, dau. of Sir Francis Hastings Doyle, 1st Bt., and d. 15
Dec. 1860.   (B.P. 1949 ed.)

TITSEY

1. All black background
Qly, 1st and 4th, Barry of eight argent and gules over all a cross patonce
sable (Gower), 2nd and 3rd, Azure three leaves or (Leveson), over all

a crescent for difference, impaling, Sable a bend between six escallops
or (Foljambe)
Crest: A wolf passant argent collared and lined or   Mantling: Gules
and argent   Mottoes: Frangas non flectes   Soyes ferme
Inscribed on frame: (dexter side) Obiit a:d: VII Kal: Jan: MCMXXIII
(sinister side) Obiit a:d: XIII Kal: Nov. MDCCCXCV
For Arthur Francis Gresham Leveson-Gower, who m. 1881, Caroline
Frederica, youngest dau. of George Savile Foljambe (hatchment at
Hazelbeach, Northants), and d. 26 Dec. 1922.   (B.P. 1949 ed.)

WALTON-ON-THE-HILL

1. Sinister background black
Barry of six ermine and azure over all a horseshoe or between three
bezants (Marshall), impaling, Argent three talbots' heads erased sable
langued gules between nine cross crosslets gules (Hall)
Cherub's head above shield
For Alice Ruth, younger dau. of the Rev. Ambrose Willliam Hall, of
Walton-on-the-Hill, Surrey, who m. 1867, George William Marshall,
Rouge Croix Pursuivant, of Ward End House, Warwickshire, and
d. 9 Nov. 1870.   (B.L.G.; M.I. Sutton church)

2. Sinister background black
Argent three talbots' heads erased sable between nine cross crosslets
gules, a crescent for difference (Hall)   In pretence: Or a chevron
between three lions' gambs erect and erased gules (Powell)
Motto: In coelo quies   Shield suspended from a bow of ribbon
flanked on each side with a festoon and a cherub's head
For Anne, dau. of Haslett Powell, who m. 1762, Ambrose Hall, and
d. 27 Jan. 1812, aged 77.   (B.L.G. 7th ed.)

3. All black background
Hall, as 2.   In pretence: Powell
Crest: A lion's head erased argent langued gules   Mantling: Gules
and argent   Motto: In coelo quies   Skull below
For Ambrose Hall, d. 31 Dec. 1815, aged 77.
(M.I. in Sutton churchyard)

WONERSH

1. All black background
Qly of eight, 1st Azure a maunch ermine over all a bend gules (Norton),
2nd, Argent a chevron between four cushions lozengewise sable
(Norton), 3rd, Argent a bend engrailed between six martlets sable

(Tempest), 4th, Gules two bars and in chief three molets argent
(Washington), 5th, Gules a chevron between three harts' heads cabossed
or (Hertford), 6th, Argent a bend engrailed sable charged in chief with
an escallop or (Radcliffe), 7th, Sable a saltire argent (Rilleston), 8th,
Argent a fess between three escallops sable (Rilleston)   In pretence:
Sable two bars gemel or, on a chief or three arrowheads points upwards
sable (Midgley)
Baron's coronet   Crest: A Moor's head affronté proper wreathed at
the temples with ivy vert and round the neck with a torse argent and
azure   Motto: Avi numerantur avorum   Supporters: Dexter, A
lion argent langued gules ducally gorged or pendent therefrom by a
riband gules an escutcheon of Norton   Sinister, A griffin argent
gules ducally gorged or pendent therefrom an escutcheon of Norton
All on a mantle gules and ermine
For William, 2nd Baron Grantley, who m. 1791, Anna Margaretta, dau.
of Jonathan Midgley, of Beverley, Yorkshire, and d.s.p. 12 Nov. 1822.
(B.P. 1949 ed.)

2. As 1, but chief argent on Midgley coat, no mantle, and with a
cherub's head in the base
Probably for Anna Margaretta, wife of William, 2nd Baron Grantley.
She d. 23 Apr. 1795.   (B.P. 1949 ed.)

3. **Dexter background black**
Norton, impaling, Per fess azure and ermine a pale counterchanged, on
the azure three eagles displayed two and one or, over all on a chevron
gules a knight's helm proper between two chaplets or (Federigo)
Baron's coronet   Crest, mantle, motto and supporters: As 1.
For Thomas Brinsley, 4th Baron Grantley, who m. 1854, Maria Chiara
Elisa, dau. of Signor Federigo, of the Island of Capri, and d. 24 July
1877.   (B.P. 1949 ed.)

4. **Sinister background black**
Argent a bend wavy sable (Wallop), impaling, Azure a maunch argent
over all a bend gules (Norton)
Countess's coronet   Supporters: Two goats sable   All on a
mantle gules and ermine
For Grace, dau. of Fletcher, 1st Baron Grantley, who m. 1799, as his
1st wife, John Charles, 3rd Earl of Portsmouth, and d. 15 Nov. 1813.
(B.P. 1949 ed.)

SUSSEX

by

Cecil R. Humphery-Smith, F.S.A.

Arundel 3: For Henry Charles, 13th Duke of Norfolk, 1856
(Photograph by Mrs. M.R. Froggatt; by permission of His Grace the Duke of Norfolk

INTRODUCTION

Over a period of more than twenty years, when I was young, I cycled through the lanes of the county of Sussex in search of coats of arms and heraldic devices. I paid many visits to the churches and houses of that most lovely of provinces in the South. Some 800 religious buildings lie on the Weald and nestle between the Downs. They yielded a feast of heraldic material, but comparatively few hatchments, and to discover why this should be so in a county the size of Sussex one must study the background of its social and religious history.

There are 305 ancient parishes in Sussex and about as many great estates and houses from which stemmed those families that might celebrate funerals with the use of heraldic displays. There is no doubt that they did. There are a good number of funeral certificates for Sussex families that had their obsequies marshalled officially by the heralds. These interesting documents survive among the records of The College of Arms. Locally, less skilled craftsmen produced the achievements and furnishings, some without authority.

A good many hatchments are recorded in the collections made by Sir William Burrell[1] and the Rev. William Hayley[2] which have long since disappeared. When the late Brigadier-General Fane Lambarde[3] came to make his survey of Sussex church heraldry in the 1920s few remained. Watercolours and drawings of Sussex churches in the Sharpe collection, as well as the splendid drawings and paintings of S. H. Grimm in the Burrell collection, clearly demonstrate the lot of the majority of Sussex churches by the end of the 18th century. Trees and vegetation were growing from most roofs, damp and dereliction had left all edifices and their contents in a sorry state. Parsons had little interest and less funds to care for the repair of the churches which were supposedly the centres of their parochial cures. Nonconformity was in vogue and few country parsons of the Established Church wished to disturb their sinecures by protesting or competing. By the late 1850s R. H. Nibbs' illustrations[4] are able to show the better states of many churches, but by then serious decay had taken its toll and fragile canvases had not survived to be restored by the reforming elements in the Church who had new-found wealth from industrialists.

Here are recorded 114 surviving, or recently surviving hatchments. In view of the vicissitudes through which many of them have passed, it is perhaps even surprising that there are so many. The oldest of those which have been identified is at Chiddingly, for Thomas Bromfield, who died in 1710; the most recent is at Northiam, for Admiral of the Fleet Sir John Byng Frewen who died in 1975.

Finally, I would not wish to miss this opportunity of paying tribute to the memory of my dear master in the craft, the late Hugh Stanford London, sometime Norfolk Herald of Arms Extraordinary, who guided me into the treasure house of armory as a youth and to say thank you to my beloved wife who has accompanied me on many a Sussex heraldic expedition when we lived in that county and since, through which work we met — heraldry was ever romantic! I am also very grateful to Peter Summers, Peach Froggatt, and John Titterton, who have done much necessary checking and have added the blazons of a number of hatchments which had not previously been recorded.

Cecil R. Humphery-Smith, F.S.A.
Northgate, Canterbury

1. British Library Manuscripts, Additional 5670-5711.
2. Sussex Archaeological Collections, Vol. IX, 356 et seq. and Vol. XXXVII and British Library Additional Manuscripts 6343-6361.
3. S.A.C. Vols. LXVII, pp. 149-187; LXVII, pp. 210-240; LXIX, pp. 190-221; LXX, pp. 134-164; LXXI, pp. 134-170; LXII, pp. 218-242; LXXIII; pp. 102-144; LXXIV, pp. 181-268, and LXXV pp. 171-189.
4. The Churches of Sussex, 1851, re-issued with text by M. A. Lower, 1852.

ALDINGBOURNE

1. All black background
Sable a chevron between three chaplets argent, in chief a molet argent
for difference (Buckle), impaling, Buckle (no molet)
Crest: From a ducal coronet or a demi-ounce proper   Mantling:
Gules and argent   Motto: Nil temere tenta nil timide
For Matthew Buckle, of Norton House, who m. Hannah, dau. of
Admiral Matthew Buckle, and d. 16 Mar. 1837. She d. 3 Aug. 1836.
(B.L.G. 1937 ed.)

ALFRISTON

1. All black background
Azure three quatrefoils argent (Vincent)
Crest: From a ducal coronet or a wolf's head proper   Mantling:
Gules and argent   Motto: Mors mihi lucrum
For Richard Vincent, who d. 1733.   (Church guide)

ARUNDEL, The Fitzalan Chapel

1. Dexter background black
Qly, 1st, Gules a bend between six cross crosslets fitchy argent, the
Augmentation of Flodden (Howard), 2nd, Gules three lions passant
guardant in pale or, in chief a label of three points argent (Brotherton),
3rd, Chequy or and azure (Warren), 4th, Gules a lion rampant argent
(Mowbray) Batons of the Earl Marshal in saltire behind shield
On dexter of main shield, an escutcheon, Azure a bull's head couped
between three estoiles argent (Coppinger)   On sinister of main shield,
an escutcheon, Gules three strirrups leathered and buckled or
(Scudamore)
Duke's coronet   Crest: On a chapeau gules and ermine a lion statant
guardant tail extended or ducally gorged argent   Motto: Sola virtus
invicta   Supporters: Dexter, A lion argent langued gules   Sinister,
A horse argent in its mouth a slip of oak fructed proper   All on a
mantle gules and ermine
For Charles, 11th Duke of Norfolk, who m. 1st, Mariana (d. 28 May
1768), dau. of John Coppinger, and 2nd, Frances, dau. and heir
of Charles Fitzroy Scudamore, and d. 16 Dec. 1815.   (B.P. 1863 ed.)
(This hatchment is at present in store awaiting restoration)

2. All black background
Within the Garter, Qly, 1st Howard, 2nd, Brotherton, 3rd, Warren, 4th,
Mowbray   Batons of the Earl Marshal in saltire behind shield
Duke's coronet   Crests: Dexter, From a ducal coronet or a pair of
wings gules each charged with a bend between six cross crosslets fitchy
argent   Centre, As 1.   Sinister, On a mount vert a horse
passant argent in its mouth a slip of oak fructed proper   Mantle:
Gules and ermine   Motto: As 1.   Supporters: As 1.
For Bernard, 12th Duke of Norfolk, who m. 1789, Lady Elizabeth
Belasyse, and d. 16 Mar. 1842.   (Source, as 1.)

3. Dexter background black
Two oval shields   Dexter, within the Garter, Qly, 1st Howard, 2nd,
Brotherton, 3rd, Warren, 4th, Gules a lion rampant or langued azure
(Fitzalan)   Batons of Earl Marshal in saltire behind shield
Sinister, within wreath, as dexter, impaling, Qly, 1st and 4th, Barry of
eight argent and gules over all a cross patonce sable (Gower), 2nd and
3rd, Azure three laurel leaves or (Leveson)
Duke's coronet   Crests, motto and supporters: As 2.
For Henry Charles, 13th Duke of Norfolk, who m. 1814, Charlotte
Sophia, dau. of George, 1st Duke of Sutherland, and d. 18 Feb. 1856.
(Source, as 1.)

4. Identical to 3.

5. Dexter background black
Qly, 1st Howard, 2nd, Brotherton, 3rd, Warren, 4th, Fitzalan,
impaling, Sable on a chevron between three lions sejant guardant
argent three castles tripletowered sable (Lyons)   Batons of Earl
Marshal in saltire behind shield
Duke's coronet   Crest, motto and supporters: As 2.
For Henry Granville Fitzalan, 14th Duke of Norfolk, who m. 1839,
Augusta, youngest dau. of Admiral Lord Lyons, and d. 25 Nov. 1860.
(Source, as 1.)
(Hatchment painted by G. and C. Bishop, Herald Painters to the Queen,
3 Bennets Hill, Doctors' Commons)

6. All black background
On a lozenge surmounted by a duchess's coronet and within a gold
tasselled cord arranged in four Stafford knots
Qly, 1st, Howard, 2nd, Brotherton, 3rd, Fitzalan, 4th, Warren, impaling,
Lyons   Supporters: As 2.   All on a mantle gules and ermine
Underneath is the date: 22 March A:D: 1886
For Augusta, widow of Henry Granville Fitzalan, 14th Duke of
Norfolk, d. 22 March 1886.   (Source, as 1.)

7. Sinister background black
Qly, 1st, Howard, 2nd, Brotherton, 3rd, Fitzalan, 4th, Warren, impaling,

Qly, 1st, Argent a maunch sable (Hastings), 2nd, Sable on a bend argent
three molets gules (Clifton), 3rd, Argent a fess between three pheons
sable (Rawdon), 4th, Gyronny of eight ermine and gules (Campbell
of Loudoun)
Duchess's coronet   Supporters: As 2.   All on a mantle gules
and ermine fastened with cords tasselled or trimmed gules
For Flora, elder dau. of Charles, 1st Baron Donnington, who m. as his
1st wife, Henry, 15th Duke of Norfolk, and d. 11 Apr. 1887.
(Source, as 1.)

Castle

1. Dexter background black
Qly, 1st, Howard, 2nd, Brotherton, 3rd, Warren, 4th, Fitzalan, impaling,
Sable on a chevron between three lions sejant guardant argent three
castles tripletowered sable (Lyons)
Duke's coronet·   Batons of the Earl Marshal in saltire behind shield
On silk   A rectangular hatchment c. 20 ins. x 15 ins.
For Henry Granville Fitzalan, 14th Duke of Norfolk, who m. 1839,
Augusta, youngest dau. of Admiral Lord Lyons, and d. 25 Nov. 1860.
(B.P. 1963 ed.)

ASHBURNHAM

1. Dexter background black
Two shields, the dexter overlapping the sinister   Dexter, within the
Garter, Gules a fess between six molets argent (Ashburnham)
Sinister, Ashburnham, impaling, Qly, 1st and 4th, qly i. & iv. Or a lion
rampant azure (Brabant), ii. & iii. Gules three lucies hauriant argent
(Lucy), 2nd and 3rd, Argent five fusils conjoined in fess or (Percy)
Earl's coronet   Crest: From a ducal coronet or an ash tree proper
Motto: Le roi et l'estat   Supporters: Two greyhounds sable
collared and lined or   All on a mantle gules and ermine
For George, 3rd Earl of Ashburnham, who m. 2nd, Charlotte, sister of
George, 5th Duke of Northumberland, and d. 27 Oct. 1830.
(B.P. 1878 ed.)

2. Dexter background black
Ashburnham, impaling, Sable the sun in splendour between nine stars,
three, two, three and one argent (Baillie)
Earl's coronet   Crest, motto and supporters: As 1.
For Bertram, 4th Earl of Ashburnham, who m. Catherine Charlotte,
dau. of George Baillie, of Jerviswood, and d. 22 June 1878.
(B.P. 1891 ed.)

(This hatchment was also used on the death of Lady Catherine
Ashburnham, in 1953; there is another hatchment for the 4th Earl
at Barking, Suffolk)

BARCOMBE

1. Dexter background black
Qly, 1st and 4th, Sable four bars argent on a chief argent three pierced
molets sable (Medley), 2nd and 3rd, Chequy gules and or a canton
ermine over all on a bend azure a griffin's head erased or between two
martlets argent (Reynes)   In pretence: Azure a cross flory or
(?Warde)
Crest: A heraldic tiger sejant sable maned or   Mantling: Or
Motto: Post funera virtus
For Edward Medley, of Coneyburrows, son of Thomas Medley of
Friston Place, Buxted, and Susanna, dau. of Edward Reynes; he m.
Sarah, and was bur. at Barcombe 17 Dec. 1754.   (P.R.)

BOXGROVE

1. All black background
Qly, 1st and 4th, Qly argent and gules on second and third quarters a
fret or, on a bend sable* three escallops argent (Spencer), 2nd and
3rd, Sable a lion rampant argent, on a canton argent a cross gules
(Churchill), impaling, Paly of six argent and sable on a bend azure
three trefoils slipped or (Fawkener)
Crest: From a ducal coronet or a griffin's head between two wings
argent charged on the breast with two bars gules   Mantling: Gules
and argent   Motto: Dieu defend le droit   Supporters: Dexter, A
griffin per fess argent and or   Sinister, A wyvern argent   Each
collared and chained sable the collars each charged with three escallops
argent
* Shown here as a single bend extending throughout both quarters
   and charged with six escallops
For Lord Robert Spencer, 3rd son of Charles, 3rd Duke of Marlborough,
who m. Henrietta, dau. of Sir E. Fawkener, K.B., and d.s.p. 23 June
1831.   (B.P. 1949 ed.)

BURTON

1. All black background
Vert an eagle displayed argent armed and langued gules (Biddulph)

Crest: A wolf sejant argent langued gules   Mantling: Gules and
argent   Motto: In coelo quies   Skull in base
For Richard Biddulph, who d. unm. 16 Oct. 1767, aged 60.
(B.L.G. 5th ed.)

2. All black background
Vert an eagle displayed argent armed and langued gules (Biddulph)
Crest: A wolf sejant argent   Mantling: Gules and argent, ending in
streamers encircling base of shield   Motto: Resurgam (on argent
side of streamer)   Skull below
For John Biddulph, of Biddulph and Burton, who d. unm. 2 Aug. 1835.
(B.L.G. 5th ed.)

BUXTED

1. All black background
On a lozenge surmounted by a countess's coronet
Azure a fess wavy argent charged with a cross formy gules in chief
two estoiles of six points argent, on a chief argent a cormorant sable
beaked and legged gules in its beak a branch of laver inverted vert, in
chief (over line of impalement) the Badge of Ulster (Jenkinson),impaling,
Argent on a bend cotised gules three roundels argent (Bisshopp)
Supporters: Two hawks wings elevated proper, belled, beaked and
legged or, each charged with a cross formy gules   All on a mantle
gules and ermine
For Catherine, dau. of Sir Cecil Bisshopp, 6th Bt., who m. as his 2nd
wife, Charles, 1st Earl of Liverpool, and d. 1 Oct. 1827.
(B.P. 1949 ed.)

2. Dexter background black
Two cartouches   Dexter, within the Garter, Jenkinson, as 1, but
with Badge of Ulster in honour point   Sinister, within ornamental
wreath, Jenkinson, impaling to dexter, Gules on a bend argent three
trefoils slipped sable (Hervey), and to sinister, Ermine two chevrons
azure (Bagot)
Earl's coronet   Crest: A seahorse or between its paws a cross formy
gules   Motto: Palma non sine pulvere   Supporters: Two hawks
wings elevated proper belled or, each charged with a cross formy
gules   All on a mantle gules and ermine
For Robert Bankes, 2nd Earl of Liverpool, K.G., who m. 1st, 1795,
Louisa Theodosia, dau. of Frederick, 4th Earl of Bristol. She d. 12 June
1821. He m. 2nd, 1822, Mary, dau. of Charles Chester, formerly
Bagot, and d.s.p. 4 Dec. 1828.   (B.P. 1949 ed.)

3. Sinister background black
Azure a fess wavy argent charged with a cross formy gules in chief two

estoiles argent (Jenkinson)   In pretence (hiding cross on fess):
Qly, 1st and 4th, Azure a griffin passant and a chief or (Evelyn), 2nd
and 3rd, Sable a chevron between three molets argent (Shuckburgh)
Two cherubs' heads above shield
For Julia, dau. and sole heiress of Sir George Shuckburgh-Evelyn,
6th Bt., who m. 1810, Charles Cecil Cope, 3rd Earl of Liverpool, and
d. 8 Apr. 1814.   (B.P. 1949 ed.)
(There is another hatchment for her at Pitchford, Salop)

4. All black background
Jenkinson, as 1, but with Badge of Ulster in dexter chief
Earl's coronet   Crest, motto and supporters: As 2.
For Charles Cecil Cope, 3rd Earl of Liverpool, who d. 3 Oct. 1851.
(B.P. 1949 ed.)
(There is another hatchment for him at Pitchford, Salop)

3. All black background
On a lozenge surmounted by a cherub's head
Qly, 1st and 4th, Sable two bars gemel argent on a chief argent three
molets sable (Medley), 2nd and 3rd, Chequy or and gules a canton
ermine, on a bend azure a griffin's head erased between two martlets
or (Reynes)   In pretence: Or a bend between three leopards' faces
gules (Waldo)
Motto: Resurgam
For Jane, dau. of Sir Timothy Waldo, who m. George Medley, and
d. 14 Dec. 1829.   (M.I.)

CHALVINGTON

1. All black background
On a lozenge surmounted by a cherub's head
Argent three bars and a canton gules (Fuller), impaling, Gules on a
bend or a baton azure, on a chief azure between two pillars a castle
argent, masoned sable, with a golden key pendent from the gate, and
below the words 'Plus Ultra' in gold (Elliot)
Motto: Resurgam
For Anne, dau. of George Augustus, 1st Lord Heathfield, who m. John
Trayton Fuller, and d. 24 Feb. 1835.   (B.P. 1939 ed.)

CHIDDINGLY

1. All black background
Qly, 1st and 4th, Azure a lion passant guardant or (Bromfield), 2nd and

3rd, Argent a cross flory sable between four choughs proper (Offley)
In pretence, and impaling, Argent a bend between two dolphins
embowed sable (French)
Crest: A lion passant guardant or gorged with a wreath or and azure
Mantling: Gules and argent   Motto: In coelo quies
For Thomas Bromfield, of Lewes, who m. Anne, dau. of Stephen
French, and d. 27 Jan. 1710, aged 73. She d. 1697.   (M.I.)

EASEBOURNE, Cowdray Park

1. Sinister background black

Qly, 1st and 4th, Gyronny of eight sable and or (Campbell), 2nd, Or a
fess chequy argent and azure (Stewart), 3rd, Argent a galley with
sails furled sable oars in action (Lorn), impaling, Argent on a cross
gules five escallops or (Villiers)
Countess's coronet   Motto: Follow me   Supporters: Two stags
proper
For Henrietta, 2nd dau. of Sir Edward Villiers, who m. 1695, as his
2nd wife, John, 2nd Earl of Breadalbane, and d. 1 Feb. 1719/20.
(B.P. 1949 ed.)

2. All black background

Within Order of the Thistle, Qly, 1st, Azure a ship sails furled within a
double tressure flory counterflory or (Orkney), 2nd and 3rd, qly i. & iv.
Gules three cinquefoils ermine (Hamilton), ii, & iii. Argent a ship with
sails furled sable (Arran), 4th, Argent a human heart gules imperially
crowned or on a chief azure three molets argent (Douglas)
Earl's coronet   Crest: From a ducal coronet or an oak tree
penetrated transversely by a frame saw proper   Mantling: Gules
and ermine   Motto: Through   Supporters: Dexter, An antelope
argent, attired, ducally gorged and chained or   Sinister, A stag
proper, attired, ducally gorged and chained or
For George, 1st Earl of Orkney, K.T., who m. 1695, Elizabeth, eldest
dau. of Sir Edward Villiers, and d. 29 Jan. 1737.   (B.P. 1949 ed.)

EASTBOURNE

1. Dexter background black

Sable three bucks' heads cabossed argent attired or, in chief a crescent
argent for difference (Cavendish)   In pretence: Sable a lion passant
guardant or between three esquires' helmets argent garnished or
(Compton)
Earl's coronet   Crest: A serpent nowed proper   Motto: Cavendo

tutus   Supporters: Dexter, A buck proper wreathed round the neck
with a chaplet of roses alternately argent and azure   Sinister, A
dragon argent, winged, ducally gorged and chained or
For George, 1st Earl of Burlington, who m. 1782, Elizabeth, dau. and
heir of Charles, 7th Earl of Northampton, and d. 9 May 1834.
(B.P. 1949 ed.)
(There is another hatchment for the 1st Earl at Cartmel, Lancs)

2. All black background
On a lozenge surmounted by a countess's coronet
Arms: As 1.
Supporters: As 1.
For Elizabeth, widow of George, 1st Earl of Burlington, d. 7 Apr. 1835.
(B.P. 1949 ed.)

3. Sinister background black
Sable three bucks' heads cabossed argent attired or (Cavendish),
impaling, Gules on a bend between six cross crosslets fitchy argent the
augmentation of Flodden and in chief a molet gules for difference
(Howard)
Countess' coronet   Supporters: Two bucks proper each wreathed
round the neck with a chaplet of roses alternately argent and azure
All on a mantle gules and ermine
For Blanche, dau. of George, 6th Earl of Carlisle, who m. 1829, William,
2nd Earl of Burlington (later 7th Duke of Devonshire), and d. 27 Apr.
1840.   (B.P. 1949 ed.)

FLETCHING

1. Sinister background black
Qly, 1st, Azure on a fess dancetty argent between three griffins passant
or three escallops gules (Holroyd), 2nd, Azure five cinquefoils in
saltire argent (Holroyd), 3rd, Ermine on a chief gules a demi-lion
rampant or (Elwood), 4th, Azure on a fess or between three swans'
heads erased argent ducally gorged gules three cinquefoils gules (Baker),
impaling, Azure three lucies hauriant argent (Way)
Baroness's coronet   Motto: Quem te Deus esse jussit
Supporters: Dexter, A lion rampant reguardant proper   Sinister, A
horse bridled proper   All on a mantle gules and ermine
For Abigail, only dau. of Lewis Way, of Richmond, who m. 1767, as his
1st wife, John, 1st Baron Sheffield, and d. 3 Apr. 1793.   (B.P. 1963 ed.)

2. Sinister background black
Qly, as 1, impaling, Azure three pelicans vulning themselves proper,
2nd and 3rd, Gules two pieces of belt with buckles erect in pale, the
buckles upwards argent (Pelham)

Baroness's coronet   Motto: As 1.   Supporters: Dexter, as 1.
Sinister, A horse proper collared with a strap argent   All on a
mantle gules and ermine
For Lucy, dau. of Thomas, 1st Earl of Chichester, who m. 1794, as his
2nd wife, John, Baron Sheffield, and d. 18 Jan. 1797.   (B.P. 1878 ed.)

3. Dexter background black
Qly, as 1, impaling, Azure a lion passant or between three fleurs-de-lys
argent (North)
Earl's coronet   Crest: A demi-griffin sable armed and beaked or
holding between the claws a ducal coronet or   Mottoes: (above)
Nullum numen abest si sit prudentia   (below) Quem te Deus esse
jussit   Supporters: Dexter, as 1.   Sinister, A dragon sable and or
ducally gorged and chained or   All on a mantle gules and ermine
For John, 1st Earl of Sheffield (cr. 1816), who m. 3rd, 1798, Anne,
dau. of Frederick, 2nd Earl of Guilford, and d. 30 May 1821.
(B.P. 1878 ed.)

4. Sinister background black
Or a lion rampant gules langued azure charged on the shoulder with a
trefoil slipped with split stalk or, a crescent sable for difference (Field),
impaling, Argent a bordure compony or and gules (Hunt)
Crest: A demi-lion rampant gules charged on the shoulder with a trefoil
slipped or   Mantling: Gules and argent   Motto: Guard against
false friends   Winged skull in base
Probably for Mary, wife of Thomas Field, of Woodgate, Fletching,
d. 9 Dec. 1779, aged 33.   (M.I.)

GLYNDE

1. All black background
Qly of six, 1st, Azure two swords points upwards in saltire argent hilts
and pommels or a bordure engrailed argent (Brand), 2nd, Per pale azure
and or a pale counterchanged and three stags' heads erased or (Roper),
3rd, Or on a fess gules three fleurs-de-lys or (Lennard), 4th, Azure
three lions rampant or (Fiennes), 5th, Gules three escallops argent
(Dacre), 6th, qly i. & iv. Chequy or and gules (Gillesland), ii. & iii. Per
pale argent and ermine three bars gules (Moulton), impaling, Argent
a lion rampant sable langued gules in chief two sinister hands couped
gules (Crosbie)
Baron's coronet   Crest: From a ducal coronet or a tiger's head
argent, langued gules, semy of roundels gules, azure and or   Motto:
Pour bien desirer   Supporters: Dexter, A wolf argent gorged with
a spiked dancetty collar with line reflexed over the back or   Sinister,
a bull gules ducally gorged or, with a line reflexed over back, horns,

hoofs, and tuft of tail or   All on a mantle gules and ermine
For Henry Otway, 21st Baron Dacre, who m. 1806, Pyne, dau. of the
Hon. and Very Rev. Dean Crosbie, and d. 2 June 1853.   (B.P. 1878 ed.)

2. All black background
On a lozenge   Argent on a fess gules between six martlets sable two
martlets or (Hay), impaling, Qly, 1st and 4th, Azure three pelicans
vulning themselves proper (Pelham), 2nd and 3rd, Gules two pieces
of belt with buckles erect in pale the buckles upwards argent (Pelham)
Motto: Resurgam
For Elizabeth, dau. of Thomas Pelham, of Catsfield, who m. William
Hay, and d. 20 May 1793. He d. 22 June 1755.   (Berry; P.R.)
(This hatchment was until recently at Ringmer)

GORING

1. Dexter background black
Qly, 1st and 4th, Gules a lion rampant or, on a chief or three laurel
branches erect proper (Pechell), 2nd, Or a cross engrailed per pale sable
and gules (Brooke), 3rd, Argent on a fess gules between three eagles'
heads erased sable a lion passant argent between two escallops or
(Wilmot), in centre chief the Badge of Ulster   In pretence: Qly,
1st and 4th, Argent on a bend cotised gules three bezants (Bisshopp),
2nd and 3rd, Gules ten bezants and a canton ermine (Zouche)
Crests: Dexter, A lark proper   Sinister, A brock proper
Mantling: Gules and argent   Motto: Ea nostra voco
For Sir George Richard Brooke-Pechell, 4th Bt., who m. 1826,
Katherine Annabella, dau. and co-heir of Cecil, 12th Baron Zouche,
and d. 29 June 1860.   (B.P. 1949 ed.)

EAST GRINSTEAD

1. Sinister background black
Gules on a saltire argent a rose gules barbed and seeded proper (Nevill),
impaling, Qly, 1st and 4th, Azure three pelicans vulning themselves
argent (Pelham), 2nd and 3rd, Gules two pieces of belt with buckles
erect in pale proper the buckles upwards or (Pelham)
Baroness's coronet   Crest: From a ducal coronet or a bull's head
erased proper collared or   Mantling: Gules and argent   Motto:
Ne vil velis   Badges: To dexter, A rose gules barbed and seeded
proper   To sinister, A portcullis or
For Henrietta, dau. of Thomas Pelham, of Stanmer, who m. George,
17th Baron Abergavenny, and d. 31 Aug. 1768.   (B.P. 1949 ed.)

2. Sinister background black

Qly or and gules over all a bend vair (Sackville), impaling, Sable a lion passant guardant or between three esquires' helmets argent (Compton)
Countess's coronet   Motto: Tous jours loyall   Supporters:
Dexter, A leopard argent semy of roundels sable   Sinister, A dragon ermine ducally gorged and chained or
For Mary, dau. of James, 3rd Earl of Northampton, who m. Charles, 6th Earl of Dorset, and d. 6 Aug. 1691.   (B.P. 1949 ed.)

3. Dexter background black

Gules three cranes argent (Cranston), impaling, Argent on a chevron, the upper part terminating in a cross formy gules, three bezants (Newland)
Crest: A crane with its head under its wing proper   Mantling: Gules and argent   Motto: Resurgam
For Edward Cranston, of East Court, who d. 7 Jan. 1841.   (M.I.)

4. All black background

On a lozenge surmounted by a cherub's head
Arms: As 3.
For Harriet, widow of Edward Cranston, d. 5 Dec. 1861.   (M.I.)

WEST GRINSTEAD

1. All black background

On a lozenge   Sable three swords points meeting in base argent pommels and hilts or (Powlett), impaling, Azure a cross flory or (Ward)
Mantling: Gules and argent   Motto: Mors ianua vitæ
For Elizabeth, dau. of John Ward, of Champions, who m. William Powlett, and d. 14 June 1753, aged 66. He d. 2 May 1746, aged 63.
(M.I.)

HAMSEY

1. All black background

Argent a chevron engrailed between three crabs gules (Bridger)   In pretence: Argent on a chevron between three wolves' heads erased sable langued gules a leopard's face or (White)
Crest: A crab gules   Mantling: Gules and argent   Motto: In coelo quies   Skull below
For John Bridger, who m. Mary White, and d. 1784.
(per Francis Steer)

2. All black background

Bridger   In pretence: Argent a fess gules between four cotises wavy sable (Eliot)

Crest and mantling: As 1.   Motto: Mori lucrum est
For Sir John Bridger, who m. Rebecca, dau. of John Eliot, of Croydon,
and d. 15 Dec. 1816. She d. 25 Dec. 1803.   (M.I.)

3. Dexter background black
Qly, 1st and 4th, Azure a bend sinister between in chief three estoiles
of six points or and in base the stock and bar of an anchor issuant
from waves of the sea in bend sinister proper, in fess point of first
quarter the Badge of Ulster (Shiffner), 2nd and 3rd, Argent on a
chevron sable between three eagles' heads erased azure armed gules
three cinquefoils argent (Jackson)   In pretence: Qly, 1st, Argent a
chevron engrailed sable between three crabs gules (Bridger), 2nd,
Argent on a chevron between three eagles' heads erased sable three
leopards' faces or (White), 3rd, A ship sailing on the sea proper, a chief
azure the dexter charged with a cross crosslet argent the sinister with
a lion passant guardant or (Tattersall), 4th, Argent a fess gules between
four cotises wavy azure (Eliot)
Crest: An estoile of six points or   Mantling: Gules and argent
Motto: Non est mortale quod opto
For Sir George Shiffner, 1st Bt., who m. Mary, only dau. and heiress of
Sir John Bridger, and d. 3 Feb. 1842.   (B.P. 1878 ed.; M.I.)

4. All black background
On a lozenge   Arms: As 3.
For Mary, widow of Sir George Shiffner, 1st Bt., d. 1 June 1844.
(Sources, as 3.)

SOUTH HARTING

1. Dexter background black
Gules on a chevron between three ostrich feathers argent a roundel
sable, in centre chief the Badge of Ulster (Fetherstonhaugh), impaling,
Ermine fretty azure, on a fess engrailed azure three roses argent
(Bullock)
Crest: An antelope argent   Mantling: Gules and argent   Motto:
Non omnis moriar
For Sir Henry Fetherstonhaugh, 2nd Bt., who m. 1825, Mary Anne
Bullock, and d.s.p. 24 Oct. 1846, aged 91.
(Complete Baronetage)

2. All black background
On a lozenge suspended from a lover's knot
Arms: As 1.
For Mary Anne, widow of Sir Henry Fetherstonhaugh, 2nd Bt., d. 29
Jan. 1874.   (Source, as 1; National Trust Archives)

Uppark

1. Identical to South Harting 1.

HASTINGS, All Saints

1. Sinister background black
Or on a bend azure a molet between two crescents or a bordure
engrailed gules (Scott), impaling, Argent a lion rampant gules, on a
chief per fess argent and azure three molets argent (McMillan)
Motto: In coelo quies   Two cherubs' heads above
For Lillies Macmillan, who m. as his 1st wife, John Scott, merchant of
Hastings, and was bur. at All Saints, 19 Sept. 1801, aged 42.
(P.R.; J. Manwaring Baines; M.I.)

2. Sinister background black
Scott, impaling, Gules three horses courant in pale argent (Frye)
Motto: Resurgam   Two cherubs' heads above
For Charlotte Frye, who m. as his 2nd wife, John Scott, and d.
(J. Manwaring Baines)

3. All black background
Scott arms only   To dexter of main shield, Scott, impaling, Argent
a lion rampant sable, on a chief sable three molets argent (McMillan)
A.Bl.   To sinister of main shield, Scott, with in pretence, Gules
three horses courant in pale argent (Frye)   A.Bl.
Crest: A hind's head couped proper   Mantling: Gules and or
Motto: In tenebris lux
For John Scott, bur. at All Saints, 11 Mar. 1815, aged 63.
(Sources, as 1.)

4. Sinister background black
Azure two lions rampant respectant or supporting a sinister hand gules
(Kelly), impaling, Azure a chevron ermine between three griffins'
heads erased or, in centre chief a cross crosslet argent (Gardiner)
Motto: Mors janua vitæ
Unidentified

5. All black background
Per pale argent and gules, in dexter chief the Badge of Ulster (Waldegrave)
To dexter of main shield, Waldegrave, impaling, Argent a chevron
between three hinds' heads erased gules (Whitbread)   S.Bl.   To
sinister of main shield, surmounted by an earl's coronet, Waldegrave
with Badge of Ulster in dexter chief, impaling, Argent a chevron sable
ermined argent between three roses gules barbed and seeded proper

(Whitear) D.Bl.   Badge of the Order of the Bath pendent below
main shield
Earl's coronet   Crest: From a ducal coronet or a plume of ostrich
feathers, the first two argent, the third per pale argent and gules, the
last two gules   Mantle: Gules and ermine   Motto: Passes avant
Supporters: Two talbots sable eared or murally gorged argent
For William, 8th Earl Waldegrave, who m. 1st, 1812, Elizabeth (d. 1
Mar. 1843), dau. of Samuel Whitbread, of Cardington, Beds, and
2nd, 1846, Sarah, dau. of the Rev. William Whitear, and d. 24
Oct. 1859.   (B.P. 1949 ed.)

6. All black background
Qly, 1st, Per pale azure and argent on a chevron engrailed between
three annulets three escallops all counterchanged (Shadwell), 2nd and
3rd, Or a chevron dovetailed between six annulets gules (Lucas), 4th, as
1st, but per pale azure and or (Shadwell), impaling, Argent a fess
nebuly gules between three lions rampant sable (Aylwin)
Crest: A wyvern argent, wings and tip of tail or, charged on the body
with six annulets gules   Mantling: Gules and argent   Motto:
Resurgam   Skull below
For William Lucas Shadwell, D.L., who m. Miss Aylwin, of Tillington,
took the additional name of Lucas in 1811, and d. 1844, aged 79.
(J. Manwaring Baines)

7. All black background
On a lozenge decorated with fleurs-de-lys
Gules on a bend engrailed or a baton azure, on a bordure or eight
roundels gules (Elliot)
For Louisa Charlotte Elliot, who m. Walter Prideaux, of London,
goldsmith, and d. at Shovells, All Saints Street, Hastings, 22 Sept.
1963, aged 97.   (J. Manwaring Baines)
(Hatchment prepared at Mrs. Prideaux's request by Philip Cole,
formerly principal of Hastings School of Art and, on her death,
displayed outside her house before being placed in the church)

HEATHFIELD

1. Sinister background black
Gules on a bend engrailed or a baton azure, in chief a martlet argent
for difference (Eliott), impaling, Sable a fess wavy between two
estoiles of six points argent (Drake)
Two cherubs' heads above shield   Motto: Mors janua vitæ
For Anne, dau. of Sir Francis Drake, 4th Bt., who m. George Augustus
Eliott (later 1st Baron Heathfield), and d. 13 Feb. 1771.
(B.P. 1939 ed.)

2. All black background
Within Order of the Bath, Gules on a bend or a baton azure, on a chief
azure between two pillars a castle argent from the gate a golden key
pendent and under 'Plus Ultra' in gold (Eliott)
Baron's coronet   Crest: A cubit arm in armour the hand proper
grasping a scimitar argent pommel and hilt or   Mantling: Gules and
argent   Motto: Fortiter et recte   Supporters: Dexter, A ram
argent, gorged with a wreath of laurel proper   Sinister, A goat
argent similarly collared
For George Augustus, 1st Baron Heathfield, who d. 6 July 1790.
(B.P. 1939 ed.)

3. Dexter background black
Qly, 1st and 4th, Barry nebuly of six or and sable a crescent argent for
difference (Blunt), 2nd and 3rd, qly i. & iv. Per fess sable and argent
a pale counterchanged three trefoils slipped argent (Symons), ii. & iii.
Vert a bend cotised argent (Pearse), over all the Badge of Ulster,
impaling, Azure five escallops in cross or (Barker)
Crest: A sun in splendour charged with an eye issuing tears proper
Mantling: Gules and argent   Motto: Lux tua vita mea
For Sir Charles Richard Blunt, 4th Bt., who m. 1824, Sophia, dau. of
Richard Baker, M.D., and d. 29 Feb. 1840.   (B.P. 1949 ed.)

4. All black background
Qly, 1st and 4th, Or three bars nebuly sable (Blunt), 2nd and 3rd, as 3,
over all the Badge of Ulster
Crest, mantling and motto: As 3.
For Sir Walter Blunt, 5th Bt., who d. unm. 13 July 1847.
(B.P 1949 ed.; M.I.)

HORSHAM

1. Dexter background black
Sable on a fess engrailed between three whelkshells or a molet sable for
difference, in centre chief the Badge of Ulster (Shelley), impaling,
Azure a lion rampant or holding in the dexter paw a sword erect argent
pommel and hilt or between two flaunches or, each flaunch charged
with an anchor sable (Pilfold)
Crest: A griffin's head erased argent ducally gorged and beaked or
Mantling: Gules and argent   Motto: Patriarum excubitor opum
For Sir Timothy Shelley, 2nd Bt., who m. 1791, Elizabeth, dau. of
Charles Pilfold of Effingham, Surrey, and d. 24 Apr. 1844. Sir Timothy
was father of Percy Bysshe Shelley, the poet.
(B.P. 1939 ed.)

2. Dexter background black
Qly, 1st and 4th, Argent on a mount vert a gaming cock proper
(Tredcroft), 2nd, Azure a dolphin argent tailed or between three
escallops or (Scrase), 3rd, Sable a chevron between three escallops
argent (Michell), impaling, Azure a lion rampant argent (Crewe)
Crest: A cock's head erased proper   Mantling: Gules and argent
Motto: In coelo quies
For Henry Tredcroft, of Warnham, Horsham, who m. Mary, dau. of
Robert Hawgood Crewe, and d. Feb. 1844.   (B.L.G. 2nd ed.)

HURSTMONCEUX

1. Sinister background black
Or two bars gemel gules a chief indented argent (Hare), impaling, Qly,
1st and 4th, Lozengy argent and sable a bordure engrailed sable
(Shipley), 2nd and 3rd, Argent a chevron between three estoiles of
seven points sable (Mordaunt)
Motto: In coelo quies   Three cherubs' heads above and winged skull
below
For Georgiana, 4th dau. of Jonathan Shipley, Bishop of St Asaph,
who m. as his 1st wife, Francis Hare Naylor, of Hurstmonceux Place,
and d. 6 Apr. 1806.   (B.L.G. 7th ed.; M.I.)

IPING

1. All black background
Qly, 1st and 4th, Gules three cinquefoils pierced ermine (Hamilton),
2nd and 3rd, Argent a lymphad sails furled sable (Arran), over all the
Badge of Ulster, impaling, Vert a chevron ermine between three wolves'
heads erased or (Wynne)
Crest: From a ducal coronet or an oak tree proper fructed or traversed
with a frame saw proper   Mantling: Gules and argent   Motto:
Sola nobilitas virtus   Pendent below shield the badge of the Order
of the Bath; also pendent, to the dexter the Crimean War
Commemorative medal, with clasps for Alma and Inkerman, and to the
sinister, another medal
For Sir Charles Hamilton, 3rd Bt., K.C.B., who m. Catherine Emily,
dau. of William Wynne, of Dublin, and d. 23 Jan. 1892, aged 81.
(B.P. 1949 ed.; M.I.)
(There is an identical hatchment at Stedham)

KIRDFORD

1. Dexter background black
Sable ermined argent on a cross quarterpierced argent four millrinds

sable (Turnour), impaling, in chief, Azure three arrows points
downwards two and one or (Archer), and in base, Gules three dexter
arms vambraced argent (Armstrong)
Earl's coronet   Crest: A lion passant guardant argent holding in the
dexter paw a millrind sable   Mantle: Gules and ermine   Motto:
Esse quam videre   Supporters: Two lions argent semy of millrinds
sable   Winged skull below
For Edward, 1st Earl Winterton, who m. 1st, Anne (d. 20 June 1775),
dau. of Thomas, 1st Lord Archer, and 2nd, Elizabeth (d. 1 Dec. 1841),
dau. of John Armstrong, of Godalming, and d. 20 Aug. 1788.
(B.P. 1949 ed.)

2. Dexter background black

Turnour, impaling to the dexter, a blank, and to the sinister, a blank,
presumably for Chapman and Board
Earl's coronet   Crest, mantle, motto and supporters: As 1.
For Edward, 2nd Earl Winterton, who m. 1st, Jane (d. 1792), dau. of
Richard Chapman, of London, and 2nd, Harriet, dau. of William
Board, of Paxhill, and d. 25 Apr. 1831.   (B.P. 1949 ed.)

LEWES, All Saints

1. Dexter background black

Qly, 1st and 4th, Argent on a chevron between three griffins' heads
erased sable three cinquefoils argent (Spencer), 2nd and 3rd, Azure on a
chevron argent three pheons gules in dexter chief a sun in splendour or
(Johnson), impaling, Azure on a chevron engrailed argent three bucks'
heads couped gules a chief per fess sable ermined argent and ermine
(Woodroffe)
Crest: A cock argent combed and wattled gules on the breast drops of
blood proper   Mantling: Gules and argent   Motto: Resurgam
Unidentified

2. All black background

Three coats per pale   Dexter, Qly, 1st and 4th, Per pale indented
argent and sable, 2nd and 3rd, Azure a fleur-de-lys or (Warner)   Centre,
Argent on a cross sable a cross fusilly ermine (Freville)   Sinister,
Argent a squirrel sejant gules cracking a nut or (Hartford)
Crest: A double plume of six feathers, three over three argent
Mantling: Gules and argent   Motto: Resurgam
Unidentified

Westgate Chapel

1. Dexter and top sinister background black

Qly, 1st and 4th, Argent a saltire engrailed between four roses gules

(Napier), 2nd and 3rd, Or on a bend azure a molet of eight points
between two crescents or within a double tressure flory counterflory
azure (Scott), impaling, in chief, Azure a chevron or between three
bezants (Hope), and in base, Argent a saltire sable on a chief gules three
cushions or (Johnston)   Shield resting on top of an embattled
tower proper
Baron's coronet   Crest: A dexter hand and wrist proper holding a
crescent argent   Mantling: Or (slight)   Motto: Ubi tua o mors
victoria   Supporters: Dexter, An eagle proper   Sinister, A
soldier in armour proper holding a spear with a pennon azure
For Francis, 6th Baron Napier, who m. 1st, Henrietta, dau. of Charles,
1st Earl of Hopetoun, and 2nd, Henrietta Maria, dau. of George
Johnston, of Dublin, and d. 1773.   (B.P. 1949 ed.)

2. Dexter third and sinister third background black
Qly of eight, 1st, Argent a chevron between three annulets gules
(Goring), 2nd, Argent three bars sable, on a canton sable a lion's face
or (Radmylde), 3rd, Argent on a chief gules three roundels two and
one argent (Camoys), 4th, Per fess dancetty gules and argent in chief
three molets argent (Dyke), 5th, Argent three lions passant between
two bendlets sable (Hawtrey), 6th, Gules on a fess ermine between
three martlets in pale two and one argent an annulet gules for
difference (Covert), 7th, Azure three pelicans in their piety argent
(Pelham), 8th, Azure fretty argent (Scures)
Crest: A lion rampant guardant sable langued gules   Mantling:
Gules and argent   Inscribed on hatchment below shield: HENRY
GORING Knight 1583   On sinister side, in small letters: G. Gordon
Godfrey pinxit A.D. 1927 .
(This hatchment was repainted in 1927 and, in some details, altered.
It was certainly not used for Sir Henry Goring but is very much later)

NORTHIAM

1. Sinister background black
Ermine four bars azure in chief a demi-lion rampant issuant gules
(Frewen), impaling, Per pale azure and sable three fleurs-de-lys or
(Jenkyns)
Crest: A demi-lion rampant or collared gules holding in his paws a
caltrap azure   Mantling: Azure and argent   Motto: Christo
duce vincam
For Sarah, dau. of the Rev. David Jenkyns, who m. Morton John
Edward Frewen, and d.   He. d. 1871.   (B.L.G. 2nd ed.)
(This hatchment, last recorded in 1962, is now missing)

2. Sinister background black
Ermine four bars azure in chief a demi-lion rampant issuant proper

(Frewen) In pretence: Argent on a chevron sable between three
squirrels sejant cracking nuts proper three acorns proper (Woodgate)
Crest: A demi-lion rampant argent collared gules holding in his paws a
caltrap azure   Mantling and motto: As 1.
For Frances, dau. of Henry Woodgate, of Pembury, who m. 1856,
Charles Hay Frewen, and d. 9 Feb. 1867. He d. 1 Sept. 1878.
(B.L.G. 1937 ed.)

3. Sinister background black

Qly of six, 1st, Frewen as 1, 2nd, qly i. & iv. Argent a cross crosslet
fitchy sable (Scott), ii. & iii. Azure three congers' heads erased two and
one or (Conghurst), 3rd, qly i. & iv. Argent on a fess azure between
six cross crosslets fitchy sable a rose argent (Laton), ii. & iii. Argent on
a chief azure three eagles' heads erased argent (   ), 4th, qly i. & iv.
Gules a saltire between four horses' heads erased or (Clarke), ii. & iii.
Azure a chevron between three leopards' faces or (Berley), 5th, qly
i. & iv. Azure three cinquefoils argent (Fraser), ii. & iii. Barry of six
ermine and gules (Gifford), over all an escutcheon, Argent three
escutcheons gules (Hay) within a bordure compony argent and azure,
6th, Ermine on a cross sable five millrinds argent (Turner), impaling,
Qly, 1st and 4th, qly i. & iv. Argent three griffins' heads couped sable
(Wilson), ii. & iii. Azure on a chevron engrailed or between nine
quatrefoils six and three argent three molets gules (Carus), 2nd and
3rd, Per pale or and vert on a chevron between three fleurs-de-lys three
cross crosslets counterchanged (Shipphard)
Cherub's head above shield
For Anne, youngest child of William Wilson Carus Wilson, of Casterton
Hall, Westmorland, who m. 1832, as his 1st wife, Thomas Frewen, of
Brickwall House, and d. 18 Feb. 1844.   (B.L.G. 1937 ed.)

4. Dexter and top sinister background black

Qly of nine, 1st, Frewen, as 1, 2nd, Turner, 3rd, Scott, 4th, Conghurst,
5th, Argent a fess between six cross crosslets fitchy sable (Laton),
6th, Argent on a chief sable three eagles' heads erased argent (   ),
7th, Gules a saltire or between four horses' heads couped argent
(Clarke), 8th, Berley, 9th, Fraser quartering Gifford with Hay in
pretence, within a bordure compony argent and azure, impaling, in
chief, Qly, 1st and 4th, Wilson, 2nd, Carus, 3rd, Shipphard, impaling,
in base, Qly of six, 1st and 6th, Vert a chevron between three pheons
argent (Homan), 2nd, Azure a fess between three lozenges or (Hyde),
3rd, Argent a lion passant gules, on a chief gules three battleaxes
argent (Jackson), 4th, Argent a cross flory voided purpure (Pilkington),
5th, Argent a cross flory gules between four martlets azure (   )
Crests: Dexter, A demi-lion rampant or collared gules holding in the
dexter paw a caltrap azure·   Sinister, A lion passant argent holding
in the dexter paw a millrind argent   Mantling: Azure and argent
Motto: Mutare non est meum

For Thomas Frewen, of Brickwall House, who m. 1st, Anne, youngest
dau. of William Wilson Carus Wilson, and 2nd, Helen Louisa (d. 1901),
dau. of Frederick Homan, of Arden Wood, co. Kildare, and d. 14
Oct. 1870.   (B.L.G. 1937 ed.)

5. Identical to 4.
(In the possession of Mr. Laton Frewen)

6. All white background
Within the Order of the Bath, with badge pendent below, Ermine four
bars azure in chief a demi-lion issuant gules langued azure (Frewen)
Crest: A demi-lion rampant argent holding between the paws a caltrap
azure   Mantling: Gules and argent   Motto: Mutare non est
meum   Supporters: Dexter, A bear proper navally gorged or
Sinister, A talbot azure navally gorged or
For Admiral of the Fleet Sir John Byng Frewen, G.C.B., who d.
30 Aug. 1975.

PETWORTH House

1. All black background
Qly, 1st and 4th, Azure a chevron between three lions' heads erased
or (Wyndham), 2nd and 3rd, Ermine two bars sable on each three
molets or (Hopton)
Earl's coronet   Crest: A lion's head erased or within a fetterlock,
the bow countercompony or and azure, the lock or   Mantling:
Gules and argent   Mottoes: Au bon droit   ISAIAH.C.32.V.8
Supporters: Dexter, A lion azure, wings inverted or   Sinister, A
griffin wings inverted argent gutty gules   Winged skull in base
For George O'Brien, 3rd Earl of Egremont, who d. unm. 11 Nov. 1837.
(B.E.P.)

2. Sinister background black
Azure a chevron between three lions' heads erased or a bordure wavy
or (Wyndham), impaling, Barry nebuly of six or and sable (Blunt)
Baroness's coronet   Supporters: Dexter, A lion azure, langued
gules, wings inverted and plain collared or   Sinister, A griffin argent
gutty and plain collared gules
For Mary Fanny, dau. of the Rev. William Blunt, of Crabbett, Sussex,
who m. George, 1st Baron Leconfield, and d. 23 May 1863.
(B.P. 1963 ed.)

RINGMER

1. All black background
Argent on a fess gules between six martlets sable two martlets or (Hay)

No helm, crest or mantling   Motto: Resurgam
Probably for Thomas Hay, M.P. for Lewes, 1768, d. unm. 9 Feb.
1786.   (Berry)

2. All black background
On a lozenge surmounted by a skull   Hay arms only
Motto: Resurgam
Probably for Frances Hay, last of the family, d. 1803.   (Berry)

RYE

1. Sinister background black
Argent a lion rampant and a canton sable (Owen)   In pretence:
Qly, 1st and 4th, Azure a lion rampant or (   ), 2nd and 3rd, Gules
three tilting spears erect two and one argent (Amherst)
Crest: Two eagles' heads and necks erased and addorsed or   Motto:
Finis coronat opus   Spray of leaves on either side of shield and
winged skull below
Unidentified

SALEHURST

1. Sinister background black
Chequy argent and gules a chief indented azure (Micklethwait)   In
pretence: Azure on a chevron or between in chief two estoiles of six
points and in base a lion rampant argent three roundels gules (Corthine)
Cherub's head above and skull below
For Jane, dau. of Josiah Corthine, of Anlaby, Yorks, who m. John
Micklethwait, and d. 12 Aug. 1819, aged 65.   (M.I.)

2. All black background
Arms: As 1.
Crest: A griffin's head argent beaked or erased gules gorged with a
collar chequy argent and gules   Mantling: Gules and argent
Motto: Favente numine
For John Micklethwait, who d. 20 Apr. 1824, aged 67.   (M.I.)

3. All black background
On a lozenge surmounted by a cherub's head
Ermine a chief quarterly or and gules (Peckham)
Motto: In coelo quies   Cherub's head above and winged skull below
For Mary Peckham, d. 6 Mar. 1779.   (M.I.; note below hatchment gives
ascription to Anne Peckham, d. 21 Jan. 1758, but the date 1779 is
inscribed in apparently contemporary Arabic numerals on the back of
the canvas)

4. All black background
On a lozenge surmounted by a cherub's head
Qly or and gules in the first quarter an eagle displayed vert (Pakenham)
Motto: Resurgam
For Elizabeth Lucretia Pakenham, of Bernhurst House, Hurst Green,
who d. unm. 1800.   (B.P. 1949 ed.; note below hatchment)

SEDLESCOMBE

1. Sinister background black
Sable a pheon argent within a bordure or charged with eight roses
argent barbed and seeded proper (Sharpe), impaling, Gules on a bend
or three martlets sable (Brabazon)
Motto: Resurgam
Shield suspended from a bow of blue ribbon with a cherub's head at
each top corner
For Anne Mary, dau. of Sir Anthony Brabazon, who m. Hercules
Sharpe, and d. 12 July 1838, aged 50. He d. 1 Feb. 1858.   (M.I.)

SENNICOTTS

1. Dexter background black
Argent a battlemented tower between three keys wards upwards and to
dexter azure, in chief a martlet sable for difference (Baker), impaling,
Argent on a fess raguly azure three fleurs-de-lys or, in chief a trefoil
slipped gules (Woods)
Crest: A branch erect vert bearing six roses argent   Mantling: Gules
and argent   Motto: Resurgam
For Charles Baker of Sennicotts House, who d. 26 July 1839.
(M.I. with arms as hatchment)

2. All black background
On a lozenge surmounted by a lover's knot with cherubs' heads at
either side and in base
Arms: As 1.
For Mary, widow of Charles Baker, d. 12 Jan. 1840.   (Source, as 1.)

3. Dexter background black
Sable a thistle or between three pheons argent (Teesdale), impaling,
Or ermined sable a fess embattled cotised gules, in chief a tripletowered
castle sable (Lautour)
Crest: From a ducal coronet or a dexter arm erect, embowed in armour
sable garnished or grasping an arrow pointing to dexter proper
Mantling: Gules and argent   Motto: Resurgam

For Christopher Teesdale, who m. Barbara, dau. of Joseph Francis de Lautour, and d. 27 Apr. 1855.   (M.I.; B.L.G. 18th ed.)

4. All black background
On a lozenge surmounted by a lover's knot with cherubs' heads at either side and in base
Arms: As 3.
For Barbara, widow of Christopher Teesdale, d. 2 Feb. 1862.
(Sources, as 3.)

SLAUGHAM

1. Sinister background black
Qly, 1st and 4th, Ermine on a chevron between three dolphins sable a roundel between two fleurs-de-lys argent, 2nd and 3rd, Argent on a chevron between three dolphins sable a roundel between two fleurs-de-lys argent (Sergison), impaling, Argent on a chevron between three moors' heads couped proper wreathed at the temples argent and sable the lowest head between two sprays of ivy proper three roses argent barbed and seeded proper (Ives)
Motto: Resurgam   Shield suspended from a bow of blue ribbon with a cherub's head at each top corner
For Janette Elizabeth, dau. of Jeremiah Ives, of Norwich, who m. as his 1st wife, the Rev. William Thomas Sergison, Rector of Slaugham, and d. 10 May 1846, aged 30.   (B.L.G. 1937 ed.; M.I.)

SOUTHWICK

1. Dexter background black
Argent a chevron engrailed between three talbots' heads erased azure langued gules, on a chief azure three molets or (Hall), impaling, Or on a chief sable three escallops or (Graham)
Crest: A talbot's head erased argent langued gules collared counter-compony argent and azure rimmed or   Mantling: Gules and argent
Motto: Resurgam
For John Hall, of Portslade, who d. 29 Dec. 1840, aged 76. His wife, Sarah, d. 31 Jan. 1842, aged 72.   (M.I.)

STEDHAM

1. Identical to Iping, q.v.
For Sir Charles Hamilton, 3rd Bt., who m. Catherine Emily, dau. of William Wynne, of Dublin, and d. 23 Jan. 1892, aged 81.
(B.P. 1949 ed.; M.I.)

STEYNING

1. All black background
Or a chevron barry of six gules and sable (Proud)
Crest: A cross calvary or   Mantling: Gules and argent
Base of hatchment inscribed: Joseph Proud
For the Rev. Joseph Proud, Vicar of Steyning, who d. 17 July 1701.
(M.I.)

STOPHAM

1. Dexter background black
Qly of eight, 1st, Sable three falconers' sinister gloves tasselled or
(Barttelot), 2nd, Qly per fess dancetty argent and gules four crescents
counterchanged (Stopham), 3rd, Azure three chevrons and in chief a
martlet argent (Lewknor), 4th, Gules three stags' heads cabossed
argent (D'Oyly), 5th, Azure two bars gemel and in chief a lion passant
guardant or (Tregoz), 6th, Or on a chief gules three roundels argent
(Camoys), 7th, Argent three cranes' heads sable (Walton), 8th,
Argent a doubleheaded eagle displayed sable (Syheston), impaling,
Argent three chaplets vert flowered gules (Woodbridge)
Crests: Dexter, A swan couchant wings expanded argent   Sinister,
A tower masoned proper   Mantling: Sable and argent
Motto: Mature
For George Barttelot, who m. 1819, Emma, dau. of James Woodbridge,
of Richmond, Surrey, and d. 28 Nov. 1872, aged 84.   (M.I.)

TILLINGTON

1. Dexter background black
Argent a fess between three moles sable (Mitford), impaling, Argent a
Paschal Lamb couchant gules, on a chief embattled gules three estoiles
of six points argent (Wicker)
Crest: Two hands couped at the wrist proper grasping a sword erect
argent pommel and hilt or the blade enfiled with a boar's head erased
sable   Mantling: Gules and argent   Motto: In coelo quies
For William Mitford, of Pitshill, who m. 2nd, 1745, Sarah, dau. of
John Wicker, of Horsham Park, and d. 5 Feb. 1777. She d. 9 May
1777.   (B.L.G. 1937 ed.; M.I.)

TORTINGTON

1. All black background
Gules a fess dancetty or ermined sable between three garbs or (Leeves)

In pretence: Or two wings conjoined in lure gules, on a chief azure
three martlets argent (Seymour)
Crest: On a mount vert a swan argent wings elevated charged on the
breast with three roundels sable ducally crowned and gorged with a
ducal coronet and chained or   Inscribed in base of hatchment:
Willm Leeves, Esq. died March 28 1710, aged 66.
For William Leeves, of Tortington Place, who m. Anne Seymour,
and d. 28 Mar. 1710, aged 66.
(B.L.G. 2nd ed.; inscr. on hatchment)

2. Dexter background black
Qly, 1st and 4th, Gules a fess dancetty ermine between three garbs or
(Leeves), 2nd and 3rd, Seymour, impaling, Or three roundels azure
each charged with a fret or (Gratwicke)
Crest: As 1.   Inscribed in base of hatchment: Richard Leeves,
Esq. died Feb. 20th, 1737, aged 50.
For Richard Leeves, of Tortington Place, who m. Mary, dau. of William
Gratwicke, of Ham, and d. 20 Feb. 1737, aged 50.   (Sources, as 1.)

TROTTON

1. All black background
Argent two bars sable on a canton sable a cinquefoil or (Twyford)
In pretence: Argent two grosing irons in saltire sable between four
Kelway pears proper all within a bordure engrailed sable (Kelloway)
Crest: A demi-lion doublequeued sable gutty or in his dexter paw a
cinquefoil or   Mantling: Gules and argent   Motto: Veritas
For Samuel Twyford, of Trotton Place, who m. Susannah (Kelloway),
and d. 26 Mar. 1826, aged 60.   She d. 5 Jan. 1795, aged 28.   (M.I.)

WALDRON

1. Dexter background black
Or on a saltire azure between two water bougets in the flanks sable
nine lozenges or (Dalrymple)   In pretence: Argent three bars
gules a canton ermine (Apsley)
Crest: A rock proper   Motto (below shield): Firm
Bugles, battleaxes, spears, cannons and flags in saltire behind shield
Probably for James Dalrymple, of Mayfield, who d. 29 Mar. 1781,
aged 49.   Cordelia, his wife, d. 6 Dec. 1802, aged 70.   (M.I.)

2. All black background
Qly, 1st and 4th, Or on a saltire azure nine lozenges or (Dalrymple),

2nd and 3rd, qly i. & iv. Apsley, ii. Argent three bars and a canton
gules (Fuller), iii. Or a cross patonce between four martlets azure
(Offley)
Crest: A rock proper   Mottoes: (above crest) Firm
(below shield) Resurgam
Unidentified

WARBLETON

1. Sinister background black

Gules two bars or (Harcourt)   In pretence: Azure on a chevron
argent three molets sable (Roberts)
Crest: From a ducal coronet or a peacock proper   Motto: Gesta
verbis praevenient   No helm or mantling   Palm branches in
saltire behind shield and winged skull in base
A small hatchment, c. 2 ft. x 2 ft.
For Martha Roberts, who m. the Rev. Henry Harcourt, Rector of
Warbleton, and d. 19 Sept. 1796, aged 79.   (M.I.)

2. All black background

Qly, 1st and 4th, Harcourt, 2nd and 3rd, Sable on a chevron between
ten martlets argent winged sable five roundels sable, on a canton or a
rose per pale gules and argent crowned or (Beard)   In pretence:
Azure on a chevron argent three molets sable (Roberts)
Crest and motto: As 1.   No helm or mantling   Palm branches in
saltire behind shield and winged skull in base   A small hatchment,
c. 2 ft. x 2 ft.
For the Rev. Henry Harcourt, Rector of Warbleton, who d. 21 Aug.
1800, aged 71.   (M.I.)

WARMINGHURST

1. Sinister background black

Qly, 1st and 4th, Azure three covered cups or (Butler), 2nd and 3rd,
Per pale or and azure on a chief gules three leopards' faces or
(Caldicott), impaling, Or a griffin segreant sable (Morgan)
Motto: In caelo quies   Cherub's head above and skull below
For Katherine, dau. of John Morgan of Tredegar, who m. as his 1st wife,
John Butler, and was bur. 25 Oct. 1748.
(Commoners, Vol. III, 518; M.I.)

2. Dexter background black

Qly, 1st and 4th, Butler, 2nd and 3rd, Per pale or and azure on a chief

gules three leopards' faces or (Caldicott), impaling, Sable on a chevron
between three cranes argent three escallops sable (Browne of Steyning)
Crest: An arm embowed sleeved azure cuffed argent the hand proper
holding a covered cup or   Mantling: Gules and argent
Motto: Ictus sed non victus
For John Butler, who m. 2nd, Mary, dau. of John Browne, of Steyning,
and was bur. 3 Jan. 1767.   (Church guide)

3. Dexter background black
Qly, 1st and 4th, Butler, 2nd and 3rd, Per pale ermine and azure, on a
chief gules three acorns or (Caldicott), impaling, Sable an esquire's
helmet sable and or between three pheons argent (Dolben)
Crest and mantling: As 2.   Motto: Mors janua vitæ   Winged
skull below
For James Butler, of Warminghurst Park, who m. Martha, dau. of the
Rev. Thomas Dolben, Rector of Stoke Poges, and d. 13 Sept. 1775.
(Commoners, Vol. III, 518)

4. All black background
On a lozenge surmounted by two cherubs' heads
Qly, 1st and 4th, Butler, 2nd and 3rd, Per pale or and azure, on a chief
gules three roses or (Caldicott), impaling, Sable an esquire's helmet
between three pheons argent (Dolben)
For Martha, widow of James Butler, d. 11 Dec. 1776, aged 42.   (M.I.)
(This hatchment was in poor condition when recorded in 1952, and has
since been destroyed)

WINCHELSEA

1. Dexter background black
Sable a chevron argent between three owls proper (Prescott), impaling,
Paly of six or and sable on a bend sable a sword point downwards
argent pommel and hilt or (Saunderson)
Crest: A hand and wrist erect sleeved azure cuffed ermine the hand
holding a flaming torch proper   Mantling: Gules and argent
Motto: Resurgam
For General Robert Prescott, who was bur. 21 Dec. 1816.   (P.R.)

2. Dexter background black
Prescott   In pretence: Argent a chevron gules between three hawks
proper (   )
Crest, mantling and motto: As 1.
For Colonel Prescott, who was bur. 31 Jan. 1816.   (P.R.)

3. Dexter background black
Azure three leopards' heads couped or (Denne), impaling, Argent on

a mount vert a tree proper, on a chief azure a molet argent (Steer)
No crest   Mantling: Azure and or   Motto: Resurgam
For Richard Denne, who m. Mary, dau. of William Steer, of
Northampton, and d. Jan. 1819.   (B.L.G. 2nd ed.)
(This hatchment was recorded in 1952, but has since disappeared)

WITHYHAM

1. All black background
Within the Garter, Qly or and gules a bend vair (Sackville), impaling,
Gules on a chevron between three boars' heads erased argent three oak
trees eradicated proper fructed or (Colyear)
Duke's coronet   Crest: From a ducal coronet or an estoile of eight
points argent   Mantling: Gules and ermine   Motto: Aut
nunquam tentes aut perfice   Supporters: Two leopards argent
spotted sable
For Lionel, 1st Duke of Dorset, K.G., who m. Elizabeth (d. 12 June
1768), dau. of Lt.-Gen. Walter Philip Colyear, and d. 10 Oct. 1765.
(B.P. 1949 ed.)
(In view of the background perhaps also used for his widow)

2. All black background
Sackville arms only
Duke's coronet   Crest, mantling, motto and supporters: As 1.
Probably for Charles, 2nd Duke of Dorset, who d.s.p. 6 Jan. 1769.
(B.P. 1949 ed.)

3. All black background
Sackville   In pretence: Azure three salmon naiant in pale argent
(Sambrook)
Viscount's coronet   Crest, mantling, motto and supporters: As 1,
but leopards collared vair
For George, 1st Viscount Sackville, who m. Diana, dau. of John
Sambrooke, and d. 26 Aug. 1785.   (B.P. 1949 ed.)

4. Dexter background black
Two shields   Dexter, within the Garter, Sackville   Sinister,
Sackville, with in pretence: Argent on a chevron azure between three
roses gules three fleurs-de-lys or (Cope)
Duke's coronet   Crest, motto and supporters: As 1.   All on a
mantle gules and ermine
For John, 3rd Duke of Dorset, K.G., who m. Arabella Diana, dau. and
co-heiress of Sir Charles Cope, Bt., of Brewerne, and d. 19 July 1799.
(B.P. 1949 ed.)

5. All black background

Two lozenges   Dexter, surmounted by a countess's coronet, Argent a bend sable in sinister chief a garb gules (Whitworth)   In pretence: Argent on a chevron azure between three roses gules slipped and leaved proper three fleurs-de-lys or (Cope)   Supporters: Two eagles wings elevated sable beaked and legged or each gorged with a ducal coronet or, pendent therefrom a shield, Argent a garb gules   Sinister lozenge, surmounted by a duchess's coronet, Sackville with Cope in pretence Supporters: Two leopards argent spotted sable   All on a mantle gules and ermine

For Arabella Diana, dau. and co-heir of Sir Charles Cope, Bt., of Brewerne, who m. 1st, John, Duke of Dorset, K.G. (see 4), and 2nd, Charles, 1st Earl Whitworth, and d. 1st Aug. 1825.
He d. 12 May 1825.
(B.P. 1949 ed.; B.E.P.; M.I.)
(There is an identical hatchment at Knole, Kent; and the hatchment of Charles, 1st Earl Whitworth, is at Sevenoaks, Kent)

6. Dexter background black

Qly of six, 1st, qly i. & iv. Argent a fess dancetty sable (West), ii. & iii. Qly or and gules a bend vair in centre chief a cross crosslet counter-changed for difference (Sackville), 2nd, Azure three leopards' faces jessant-de-lys or (Cantelupe), 3rd, Gules a lion rampant between eight cross crosslets fitchy or (De La Warr), 4th, Azure four bars and in chief a lion passant guardant or (Tregoz), 5th, Argent a fess gules between three molets of six points sable (Ewyas), 6th, Gules three bendlets or (Gresley)   In pretence: Sackville
Earl's coronet   Crests: Dexter, From a ducal coronet or a griffin's head azure eared and beaked or   Sinister, From a ducal coronet or an estoile of six points argent charged for difference with a cross crosslet gules   Badges (on either side of crests): Dexter, A crampet or, the inside per pale azure and gules charged with the letter r argent Sinister, A rose per pale argent and gules   Motto: Jour de ma vie Supporters: Dexter, A wolf argent langued gules collared or Sinister, A cockatrice or winged azure

For George John, 5th Earl De La Warr, who m. 1813, Elizabeth, dau. and co-heir of John, 3rd Duke of Dorset, and d. 10 Feb. 1869.
(B.P. 1949 ed.)
(Widow's hatchment is at Knole, Kent)

7. All black background

Qly of six, 1st, qly i. & iv. West, ii. & iii. Sackville, as 6, 2nd, Cantelupe, 3rd, Gules a lion rampant between nine cross crosslets fitchy or (De La Warr), 4th, Gules two bars gemel and in chief a lion passant guardant or (Tregoz), 5th, Ewyas, 6th, Gresley

Earl's coronet   Crest, badges and motto: As 6.   Supporters:
As 6, but cockatrice also combed and wattled gules   Three crosses
pendent below shield which is surrounded by the collar of the Order
of the Bath; the centre cross is the Bath, the others the Medjidie
and the Legion of Honour
For Charles Richard, 6th Earl De La Warr, who d. 23 Apr. 1873.
(B.P. 1949 ed.)

SELECT BIBLIOGRAPHY

P. G. Summers, *How to read a Coat of Arms* (National Council of Social Service, 1967), 17–20.

P. G. Summers, *The Genealogists' Magazine*, vol. 12, No. 13 (1958), 443–446.

T. D. S. Bayley and F. W. Steer, 'Painted Heraldic Panels', in *Antiquaries Journal*, vol. 35 (1955), 68–87.

L. B. Ellis, 'Royal Hatchments in City Churches', in *London and Middlesex Arch. Soc. Transactions* (New Series, vol. 10, 1948), 24–30 (contains extracts from a herald-painter's work-book relating to hatchments and 18th-century funerals).

C. A. Markham, 'Hatchments', in *Northampton & Oakham Architectural Soc. Proceedings*, vol. 20, Pt. 2 (1912), 673–687.

INDEX